JOURNEYS OF HOPE AND REALITY

A Memoir

by

Russell C. Notar

DORRANCE
PUBLISHING CO
EST. 1920
PITTSBURGH, PENNSYLVANIA 15238

Dorrance Publishing Co
585 Alpha Drive
Suite 103
Pittsburgh, PA 15238
Visit our website at *www.dorrancebookstore.com*

ISBN: 978-1-4809-3894-6
eISBN: 978-1-4809-3871-7

This memoir is dedicated to my wife, Ellen, and my daughters, Beth and Susan, who have encouraged me in my life's work with and for cooperatives throughout the world. Also, I have appreciated the curiosity of my grandsons, Chris, Emile, and Isaac, who always wanted to know "more"!

Tuareg Cross

Tuareg crosses are from the Tuareg tribes in Mali, Africa. They have symbolic meaning to the Bella women who wear them as they are believed to be powerful talismans. They are to ward off evil, and are symbolic of power and cunning.

When they are given the blessing is bestowed by saying "I give you the four corners of the world because one cannot know where one will live, and where one will die, only that we need each other."

The cross in the background on the front cover is the Tuareg Cross.

Hope is the strongest force which moves people. A hope that transforms, that makes new realities, is that which opens the way of liberty to man. To encourage hope, it is necessary to unite courage and knowledge in all people.

Oscar Arias, President of Costa Rica

CONTENTS

INTRODUCTION

The idea of cooperation is not a new concept in human affairs. The Mayans, who built beautiful and long-lasting buildings, temples, and observatories, developed a culture and society which required that people work together for the good of all. The Pilgrims, who came to this vast wilderness on the Atlantic Ocean, depended on the Native Americans, and worked together with them to survive in the early years of their lives in this New World. Later, Scandinavian farmers came to this country, and in the upper Midwest, erected houses, barns, and cleared land together, realizing that cooperation works!

Today, in the 21st century, the cooperative model has become a trademark of success in all kinds of interesting ways in which people want to combine realism with idealism. That is, people know that they have to "earn a living" to provide food, clothing and shelter for themselves and their families. Many believe that they can accomplish those basic needs through working with others who share common goals, hopes and dreams without participating in the subscribed corporate, stockholder-owned structure. Corporate business has helped to make this a great country, and so have cooperatives!

What are several of the cooperatives which have become everyday accepted entities on the world scene? Credit unions, which were developed in Germany in the 19th century, were exported to Canada, and immigrated to the United States in the 1920's, have helped millions of small savers to gain financial security all over the world.

Agricultural marketing cooperatives, also a European tradition, have enabled farmers to form cooperatives, share information, and sell their milk, cheese, corn, wheat, beef, pork, and valued added products to grocers in the United States and overseas. Millions of people have benefited from their ability to access foodstuffs produced by cooperative agricultural businesses.

PROLOGUE

This book is being written in order to provide an understanding of my life's work—that is, a life of assisting people all over the world to embrace the cooperative model of sustainable development. It wasn't easy! The travel to remote parts of the world, the natural disasters along the way, the courageous, and fascinating characters that I worked with, and the language barriers that had to be overcome, all contributed to my experiences and adventures, and I'm glad that I'm still around to report on them!

Sustainable development is an active process, whereby those involved can "sustain" themselves and their families after an initial phase of financial and educational inputs have been completed. The cooperative model is a time-tested process of community problem identification, planning, testing of hypotheses, budgeting, job identification, projection of outputs, and sharing of costs and benefits. If this sounds like a small business model, and it is, cooperatives are not-for-profit businesses.

The emphasis inherent in the cooperative model is working together—that is, there are no stockholders only "stakeholders". From the inception of the cooperative, elected leaders must involve the membership. As the cooperative matures and produces products and/or services, which produce earnings, those earnings are shared by the members, after expenses. This description reflects the basic or early cooperative model, and as time has proven, cooperatives in the 21st century have become more sophisticated, by necessity. Yet, they have grown and prospered by adhering to the principle of participation and sharing of decisions.

There are seven principles upon which cooperatives are judged. They are:

- Voluntary and Open Membership
- Democratic Member Control
- Member Economic Participation
- Autonomy and Independence
- Education, Training and Information
- Cooperation among Cooperatives
- Concern for Community

FOREWORD

This book has been written as a memoir of my work and travels, first as an officer of NCBA, (the National Cooperative Business Association) and CLUSA (the Cooperative League of the United States of America). NCBA is the non-profit membership association of cooperatives, with offices in Washington, D.C. CLUSA is the international development arm of NCBA and was the original title of the association, which was changed in 1973. Later, I was elected President and CEO of NCBA/CLUSA and CBI (Cooperative Business International), which was the for-profit subsidiary of NCBA. CBI was established in order to assist international cooperatives, which had matured into viable business organizations, and were interested in marketing products or services around the world. Unfortunately, as a subsidiary, CBI had never been capitalized, and therefore, its financial status was dependent upon the dues generated from NCBA, which was detrimental to the success of both organizations. Developing CBI into a stand-alone entity required that it finally had to be capitalized, which meant selling stock, and that was one of my many challenges as President and CEO.

During my tenure as President, I was also charged with creating a stronger endowment for CDF (the Cooperative Development Foundation). CDF provides funding for special cooperative projects in education, personnel development and training for cooperatives domestically, and internationally. The generosity of many organizations and individuals assisted me in improving the financial base of CDF, and in turn, assisting cooperatives all around the world. I should mention that CDF is the lead organization in organizing and sponsoring the Cooperative Hall of Fame, which, each year, nominates several individuals who have been recognized for their outstanding contributions to the cooperative community. The awards ceremony is attended by over four hundred people each year, who contribute to the Cooperative Development Foundation.

This memoir is not intended to be "all inclusive"—that is, to describe all of my involvement and travels to develop and promote cooperatives. It is designed to provide understanding and insights to the challenges, successes and failures of working overseas in the 1990's. I wanted to insure that at least some of the many people and organizations who have given their talents and financial support to cooperatives are recognized. The Nationwide Insurance Company and the National Cooperative Bank are two outstanding examples of organizations which have supported NCBA through their leadership, advice and counsel. I also want to mention that other organizations including the Agency for International Development, the U.S. Department of Agriculture, the International Development Bank, and the African Development Bank were and are committed to assisting undeveloped countries in their quest for stability and some measure of prosperity. NCBA, CLUSA and CBI would not have achieved any measure of success without their support and involvement. I appreciated all of their assistance.

Finally, I want to recognize the NCBA Board of Directors and all the employees of the NCBA/CBI "family" who during my tenure were supportive of me, sometimes wondering why and how I was deviating from the strategic plan! My management style was based on walking around and listening, and when I wasn't in the office, and could do neither, my telephone messages and *urgent* faxes proliferated! It was the time before the electronic revolution had been introduced to cooperatives, and therefore, I utilized what I had. It seemed to work pretty well!

THE PHILIPPINES
1991

June, 1991
Manila, the Philippines

The original intent for the chartering of Cooperative Business International (CBI), was to initiate trade between U.S. cooperatives and cooperatives in overseas locations where NCBA had successfully developed projects which had produced products and services. CBI had not been successful for a number of reasons, including a stable financial base, for as a company, it had never been capitalized! Therefore, it continued to be supported by the membership of NCBA through it dues and grants, resulting in a fragile financial situation for both organizations. One country which had not been as dramatically affected by this financial malaise was Indonesia, primarily because Sam Filiaci, Vice President of NCBA/CLUSA, was in charge. Sam was a former Peace Corps volunteer, and had decided, early in his career, that he wanted to work overseas because he believed that's where the opportunities for personal growth were. He was a dedicated believer that the cooperative model was ideal for Indonesia. I wanted to travel there, to meet him and to determine what management techniques he was using to make Indonesia a place where its products could be desirable to U.S. companies and others around the world. But first, I wanted to meet with two contacts in Manila, whom had worked with the previous officer of CBI to determine why no success had been forthcoming there.

My flight from Hong Kong experienced heavy winds and rain, and the captain explained that we had passed the tail-end of a typhoon! As I took a taxi from the airport to my hotel in the city center, called the Makati, I noticed significant damage to businesses, homes and downed trees with flooding in many places. Also, I observed terrible poverty, with people living in tin shacks, children half dressed, unpaved streets, and animals running along the street, sometimes slowing the taxi to a standstill. I could not understand, in the country's capital city, that the trip from the airport could leave the impression of a third world country. I arrived at the hotel in the midst of a massive clean-up from the tornado, paid the taxi driver in US dollars, and was met by two soldiers with AK-47's at the entrance in front the hotel! I asked the clerk at the registration desk about the soldiers with weapons. He replied that there had been an increase in guerilla activity, even here in the capital, and the hotel was taking precautions. Late that afternoon, I met with the two men that were interested in filling me in as to why NCBA/CBI had not been successful there, and of course, they indicated one of the key reasons was the lack of understanding from the previous individual whom was no longer with the organization. We agreed to meet the next day at their offices to determine if we could salvage something for the future of coops and CBI in the Philippines.

I went to bed early, and was awakened at about 2:00 A.M. by the chest of drawers in my room toppling over and hitting the floor! I jumped out of bed and looked out the window, thinking that a truck or bomb had hit the side of the hotel, but all I saw were white fluffy flakes falling from the sky! I knew it was June in Manila, and it couldn't be snowing.. I called downstairs to the front desk, and the concierge, in a very strained voice, explained that Mt. Pinatubo, an active volcano, eighty miles north of Manila, had erupted, and ash and lava were pouring from the top of the mountain. The "snow" that I saw out my window was fly-ash from the volcano. He suggested that the dining room was open, and the hotel had back-up generators, so we still had electricity for food preparation and coffee. Most of the city was dark! This event began a strange series of unusual trials and tribulations for me in Manila.

June, 1991
The Philippines

The next several days were filled with trying to communicate with my wife, Ellen, whom was a professor at Johns Hopkins University. With NCBA/CBI Headquarters in Washington, D. C. and with Sam Filiaci in Indonesia—all to no avail! Telephone lines were down (and this was before computers, iPhones, etc.), and Manila was in extreme chaos! Fly-ash, when it is exposed to moisture/humidity (Manila is quite humid in June), or rain, hardens very rapidly and becomes like concrete. Roofs were caving in, roads became impassable, the airport runways were filled with fly-ash and were unusable, and drain pipes were tearing off houses and falling to the ground! The sewer system in the city was clogged. Taxis, and buses could not move on the streets, and the traffic lights were not working anyway! The National Guard was mobilized to prevent looting and security alarms, because of no electricity were not functioning. But Manila was not the only part of the country which was affected by Mt. Pinatubo's eruption. The US Naval Base at Subic Bay, and the US Air Force Base at Clark Field, because of their proximately to the volcano, were covered in fly-ash. About twenty-thousand military personnel and their families from these bases were taken out by navy ships to other locations in the Philippines and Hawaii. Some military personnel, who remained behind to secure these facilities, were then expected to use civilian transportation when it became available. It was estimated that almost one million natives in the central areas of the island of Luzon, mainly farmers and their families, had been affected, with thousands killed. Tremors followed the initial eruption, and then typhoon-like rains followed which caused the large volume of fly-ash and some lava to begin traveling at high speed down the hillsides claiming more lives.

The US Embassy contacted all US citizens still in the country, for there were tour groups, business people, vacationers, golfers, etc. and tried to maintain communication with those they knew about. I was invited to several meetings of the Makati Chamber of Commerce to learn first-hand about the scope of the disaster and the prospects for leaving Manila. (Later, when I arrived back in the US, I received a plaque from the Chamber indicating I had survived Mt. Pinatubo.). After nine days, the hotel (which was the Peninsula], was still functioning, and food was available, not quite with the choices that normally would be on the menu, but they were amazing to do what they did. I had heard that several planes were going to try to use the runways, so I checked out of the hotel (bad decision) and went to the airport thinking I could stand by which I had usually been successful doing in the past. The airport looked like a scene from Dante's Inferno! Several thousand people had the same idea, and it was discovered that the planes, which had tested take-offs, had sucked fly-ash into their engines and were being cleaned! The planes could not take off. I finally got a taxi back to the hotel only to find several hundred people wanting a room. Just as I was being turned away, the hotel manager came out of his office, and seeing my plight said, "Mr. Notar, thank you for your complimentary comments when you checked out this morning! We can always find a room for you." I have never failed to complete the comment card during my hotel stays since! I got a small room, which I needed for several more days, and then I tried something I had never done before or since.

Finally, on June 21st, I learned from the hotel travel agent that flights were scheduled for the next day. I wanted to go back to Washington, D. C. no matter the route; Indonesia would have to wait until next time! He said that many others wanted to leave also, *but* for a small additional fee, he might be able to arrange it. I paid a "stipend" of $100, and my old ticket was accepted. I boarded the plane on my birthday; the stewardesses had seen my passport and knew it was my birthday, and came and sang, "Happy Birthday" to me before the plane took off! The routing took forty hours through Hawaii, Los Angeles, Chicago, and finally home! But, I had quite a present, and I had survived Mt. Pinatubo!

THE AMERICAN COOPERATIVE ENTERPRISE CENTER
1990-1992

1 990-1991
The American Cooperative Enterprise Center

In the fall of 1990, former Chair of the Nationwide Insurance Companies, Frank Sollars, went to Capitol Hill in Washington D.C. to testify on behalf of US cooperative businesses and their counterparts in Central and Eastern Europe. He stated, "That more than one hundred million members of cooperatives in Europe, with a cooperative history of almost one hundred and fifty years, have not had the opportunity to demonstrate their capabilities as cooperatives for over fifty years!" He continued, "I know that the right approach is to engage American cooperatives intensively, in their development process." Frank Sollars' testimony was both accurate and prophetic. The Berlin Wall had finally been dismantled in November, 1989, and the decline of Communist influence in Central and Eastern Europe had begun years earlier. The Soviet Union had half-heartedly tried to maintain the long history of cooperative business' success in their sphere of influence with the creation of the Central Soyez group of cooperatives, which were primarily agriculture-oriented. In the 1980's, the grapevine in Western Europe noted that Central Soyez was a façade of an organization, that is, it emphasized the communist philosophy, not based in any way on the cooperative model. Therefore, cooperatives were not well led, and declined from the most serious involvement of cooperative membership and contribution, even in a planned economy. This perception, even if half true, was at the heart of Frank Sollar's testimony, and reflected his experiences as he had traveled to Europe during the Cold War period, following World War II. He believed that US cooperatives could bring hope and ultimately, a restoration of cooperative business in Europe.

By way of background information, Nationwide Insurance Company was incorporated in December, 1925, as the Farm Bureau Mutual Automobile Insurance Company, and started operations in April, 1926. The Ohio Farm Bureau had loaned the new company $10,000 for start-up operations, and named Murray D. Lincoln as executive secretary. Mr. Lincoln was one of the country's early advocates of consumer and producer cooperatives in the United States and knew that the new company could serve these businesses. He was an early supporter of Franklin D. Roosevelt, whom was focused on bringing small businesses back from the debilitating Great Depression, and met with Eleanor Roosevelt as she took the lead in forming the United Nations, which he visualized as helping small businesses overseas. He became an advocate of raising funds to buy hand plows and sending them to war-torn Europe, and other undeveloped countries. Therefore, the history of helping cooperatives and other businesses by Nationwide Insurance, not only in the US, but overseas as well, was a significant part of the company's culture, long before Frank Sollar's testimony in 1990. In early 1991, following this appearance before Congress, the National Cooperative Business Association, where Mr. Sollars was also Chairman of the Board of Directors, submitted a proposal to the United States Agency for International Development, which was designed to assist cooperative development in Central and Eastern Europe. After several meetings, and discussion with USAID, which included reshaping the proposal, a unique agreement was approved. This agreement would include funding from USAID, but also required funding from NCBA and its membership.

1990-1991

The American Cooperative Enterprise Center

Those members who pledged their time and money, included: Ag Processing, Inc., Co-Bank, Country Mark Inc., the Cooperative Development Foundation, the Center for Cooperatives at the University of Wisconsin, Farmland Industries, Nationwide Insurance, and Twenty-first Century Genetics. As noted, this project was unique in many respects and included the following objectives:

- To provide technical assistance, education, and training to cooperatives and small businesses in Central and Eastern Europe.
- To offer business opportunities to ACE Center members/partners and other businesses in joint ventures, trade, financial assistance, and other programs which bring together US and European expertise.
- To provide business opportunities to Cooperative Business International([CBI) which was a for-profit subsidiary of NCBA.

Bob Scherer, President and CEO of NCBA and CBI had his home just outside of Columbus, Ohio and was a farmer and businessman who was a personal friend of Frank Sollars. He also had many contacts at Nationwide Insurance. He led the discussion with the members noted above regarding the qualifications of who would be selected to lead this important initiative. It was decided that Peter Mishek, a marketing specialist employed by Ag Processing, Inc. in Omaha, Nebraska would be selected. He would be named a Vice President of NCBA, and would be responsible to Bob Scherer and the member/partners. My responsibilities with the international efforts of NCBA/CBI would be to monitor Mr. Mishek's progress and ensure that he had the resources that were available from the member/partners and USAID. Peter had a Czech heritage, was married

9

with three children, was college educated, and was grounded in the cooperative model. A number of meetings at NCBA's headquarters in Washington D.C. followed, in which the details of office space, equipment, living arrangements for the Mishek family, schools for two of the children, financing arrangements among the member/partners, etc. were discussed and agreed upon. Much of the implementation was linked to exactly where in Europe the Center's headquarters would be located. It was decided that several groups of the partners would travel to Europe to examine various locations, and meeting, where possible, cooperative organizations which still existed. The cities selected by the partners were: Berlin, Germany; Budapest, Hungary; Prague, Czechoslovakia; and Warsaw, Poland.

Autumn, 1991
Berlin, Germany
Berlin was still recovering from the damage of World War II, and although the Berlin Wall had been demolished in 1989, East and West Berlin had not been fully or even partially reconciled. One of my most lasting memories of our travel through Berlin, was during our walk past the Russian Embassy toward the still-damaged Reichstag, when we noticed a group of men and women holding candles with photos, in prayerful silence. At the edge of the group, we asked what the ceremony was all about. We were told that these photos were of the last people— about twenty in number—who had been killed trying to climb the Wall between East and West Berlin. The Reichstag itself was at the end of a huge open area, where thousands of Germans had cheered the Nazi spectacles, and the eerie feeling of these voices from the past still seemed to permeate the place. The next day, we met with several German coop leaders, but concluded that the rehabilitation process of Berlin and of Germany, as a nation, was in its early stages, and therefore, the Center's office would not be well-placed here.

Autumn, 1991
The American Cooperative Enterprise Center
Budapest, Hungary

Budapest was the next stop on our investigations, which was really two cities, Buda and Pest, which reside on opposite sides of the Danube River. As we discovered, the Danube, after centuries and conflicts, was no longer blue! The city was founded, as the legend describes, by the seven tribes of "early" Hungary, and these tribes are featured by a sculpture of seven fierce-looking horsemen, complete with weapons, in the main square. The Hungarian language is difficult to master and to understand, and it is said that it resembles the Finnish language, more than any other. Budapest was the focal point of the demonstrations for democracy against the Hungarian Communist Party, which turned violent when the Russian government decided to intervene with troops and tanks in October-November, 1956. Many civilians were killed and wounded, and the uprising was put down. Even in 1991, there was a simmering distrust of the United States and several of its allies, because the populace thought that the demonstrations would prompt the west to come to their aid. It didn't happen, and it would be almost thirty-five years until the Communist yoke was lifted. Based upon our meetings there, the partners felt it would not be wise to locate the Center in Budapest.

Late Autumn, 1991
Warsaw, Poland

We arrived in Warsaw as winter was approaching, and it was cold and damp, but no snow, as of yet. Our contacts in the city had arranged a meeting with local coop leaders and other interested parties at one of the US hotels, which had opened after the Cold War had begun to thaw. A conference room had been set up in a horse-shoe configuration to facilitate discussion, and we were impressed! *Except*, the conference room was on the far side of the banquet area, where food and beverages had been prepared. The area had been shut off from the main hall with two heavy doors, so that we wouldn't be disturbed. As the doors were

opened, our coop guests descended upon the buffet before any discussion was possible, and it seemed in a very short period of time, the
buffet was empty! None of our delegation had an opportunity to eat
or talk, because of the hungry crowd. Obviously, our guests had not
had an opportunity such as this, to enjoy food and drink, in a very
long time. When we did sit down at the conference table, it was apparent that the protests at the Gdansk shipyards, against Communist
rule, which actually began in 1980, long before the Berlin Wall came
down, were a proud beginning for democratic rule in Poland. Our
group had the opportunity to tour Warsaw, and we saw the infamous
Ghetto, but we also witnessed streets with war-scarred buildings, and
rubble, which the Polish government had not had the resources and
the time to begin the rehab work. Our committee concluded, much
as they had in Berlin, that any expectation of success in Warsaw would
be a long term proposition.

Late Autumn, 1991
Prague, Czechoslovakia
The Nazis invaded Czechoslovakia in 1939, early in World War II, and
demanded that the Czech government surrender or the civilian population would be annihilated and infrastructure would be demolished!
After a day of deliberation, the Nazis were in control. Although a blot
on the pride of the Czech people, the decision to surrender saved many
people, many of the beautiful buildings in the country, and especially
in Prague, the capital city. The famous Charles Bridge, over the Vltava
(Moldau) River was intact throughout the war. The world-famous
Prague Castle was not harmed, and the history of cooperative community in Prague was quite positive. Vaclav Havel had been elected president in 1990, and his reputation as the dissident writer, which
challenged Communist rule, in what became the "Velvet Revolution"
was appealing to the committee, because of the stability his election en-
gendered. After several meetings with coop leaders in Prague, it was
decided that it would be the location of the Center.

1992

The American Cooperative Enterprise Center

The Center opened August 31, 1992, with the traditional ribbon-cutting and representation of most of the NCBA members who had sponsored this historic initiative. Representatives from local cooperatives, and from USAID were also present. Bob Scherer, President and CEO of NCBA/CBI made brief remarks and introduced Peter Mishek and his family, who then conducted a tour. The Center's office was located on the ground floor of a residence, the owners of which were pleased to rent this space and to have the honor of having the Center as part of their neighborhood. The office was walking distance to a bus line, and had easy access to downtown Prague. As Peter settled into his job, he discovered that the amenities of telephone, postal service, banking, credit card use and bill payment were not what Americans were used to "back home"! For example, it took several months for a telephone to be installed because of the long waiting list for service after the years of Communist rule. No credit cards were available, primarily because there was no processing system yet in place in most of Central and Eastern Europe. Most bill paying could not be handled by mail, because the invoice system which we were used to did not exist; therefore, when the electric bill for the month was due, Peter had to drive downtown, go to a location with a large wooden door, indicate to the guard who he was, and then pay the bill in cash! US currency was preferred! As he began to make contacts in the Czech cooperative community, and beyond, he found that the years of Communist rule had undermined the initiatives of many coops which had begun to reconstitute their businesses after the end of the Second World War. He indicated to his coop contacts there, that he was bringing contacts, limited funding, and access to US cooperatives who wanted to do business in Central and Eastern Europe. As he discovered, one of the key elements he brought to his contacts was *hope*, for a new beginning!

As his outreach progressed, which included speaking to coop membership, meeting with other US business and government representatives, and representatives of the Czech government, he concluded that his marketing skills and developmental background would be severely tested in this assignment. On one hand, the local and regional coops welcomed this US initiative; on the other hand, their need for capital and funding beyond the ability of the ACE Center to provide was a constant challenge. As Peter communicated these realities to USAID and NCBA, he knew that expectations for the center would have to be revised. As he continued his efforts through several years, he had limited success as identified by the original objectives. He was able to begin a market for popcorn and related products from a US coop to Central Europe to initiate the beginning of the snack interest in Europe. He helped to organize several new agriculture-related coops near Prague, which included milk and cheese products and market garden vegetables. His presence indicated a continued US interest in assisting Europe!

The evaluation at the termination of the ACE Center Project after five years was mixed. USAID was not completely aware of the lack of "normal" support systems, which, even in the 1990's, were taken for granted in the United States. For example, telephone installation and communication was very rudimentary, rent payments and other equipment purchases had to be handled in cash because no check clearing system existed. Finally, coops were no longer part of a planned economy. A new era of cooperative development had been initiated after the expiration of the project by the ACE Center, but it would take several years for the original objectives cited for the ACE Center to have any impact on cooperative development in Central and Eastern Europe. Peter Mischer returned to AG Processing, Inc. in a management position.

INDIA AND BANGLADESH
1992

M arch, 1992
India

As Senior Vice President, International of NCBA-CLUSA and CBI, I was responsible for seeking opportunities which would take advantage of products and services produced through our contracts and grants on the cooperative side of our organizations, and link them to business opportunities for Cooperative Business International. When Bob Scherer, President at the time, asked me to take on this challenge, it was as the result of his firing of the Vice President of CBI. Let me explain, further. NCBA was the membership association of cooperatives in the United States. CLUSA (the Cooperative League of the United States of America) was the non-membership entity of NCBA, and was responsible for international development grants and contracts, often through the US Agency for International Development, the African-American Development Bank, CARE (Cooperative Assistance and Relief Everywhere), and other funding agencies. CBI had been organized in the late 1980's to develop trading opportunities but had not shown much in the way of results. Therefore, I was quite aware of the challenges ahead of me. I should mention that in my previous position as Executive Vice President of the Credit Union National Association, and for a period of time Acting President & CEO], I had traveled internationally as a result of my responsibilities with the newly formed World Council of Credit

Unions which was working with several of the agencies noted above. Credit Unions in the US *and* overseas are, of course, cooperatives! This period of time was critical for NCBA, in that the membership/domestic component was doing relatively well (which had been my initial focus after joining NCBA), but CBI was not generating income as it was designed to do, and therefore was a continuing siphon on NCBA's finances. The positive financial linkage between these two entities had not been realized.

I did not have a large staff! I had an assistant-secretary, and a gentleman, Sultan Reza, who was a Bengali, and had international experience. Therefore, we both knew that our travel schedules would be quite demanding. We began by looking at what the previous individual who had headed up CBI had accomplished or tried to initiate. The records were not very substantial, but what was immediately apparent was that he had tried to utilize his contacts with USAID, where he had worked previously, in order to develop contracts that could ultimately result in earnings, not only for the coop, but ultimately for CBI. We decided to review *current* grants and contracts on the CLUSA side of the business, to determine if near term opportunities could result in an earnings flow. It was decided that, with Mr. Reza's background, and a previous success of a cooperative milk pasteurization project in India, we would investigate opportunities there. Also, there existed in India, a relatively small, but active cooperative community which was working with the urban and rural population to provide some upward mobility to the strict caste structure. India's government was indecisive as to whether it wanted to embrace Communism, or to explore a closer relationship with the United States. In addition, the long history of Great Britain's presence and its colonial attitude toward India had its supporters and detractors of that relationship. Therefore, cooperatives had slowly emerged as an alternative for urban and rural people to join together in small businesses to support themselves on a local basis, and to begin to export tie-dyed clothing, shoes and sandals, crafts, and costume jewelry. Many Indians had emigrated to the United States and beyond and had gone into businesses that produced these consumer focused products.

March, 1992
India

Sultan and I contacted Dr. Sharma, President of the Indian Cooperative Federation, and he invited us to come to New Delhi to discuss how we could work together. He setup an initial meeting with India's Secretary of Agriculture, who greeted us with several members of his staff, all dressed in the traditional Shalwar Kameez, the white long shirt and white long fitting pants. The Secretary was enthusiastic about the possibility of our working with Indian cooperatives, but made it quite clear that no financial support would be available from India to assist Indian cooperatives! Dr. Sharma had warned us of the government's attitude, but to experience it first hand was a revelation. The Secretary went on to say that if USAID or other US funding agencies were to consider helping India, he would appreciate that! We left that meeting thinking how short-sighted his view was in attempting to help his own people. We had decided to focus on agriculture as one way to pursue the prospect of financial linkage between CLUSA and CBI and India because of the possibility of food products that could be consumed locally, and exported, we believed that this approach would complement the milk project cited earlier. While we were in New Delhi, Dr. Sharma arranged for us to visit several of the clothing and craft cooperatives which were located there. As we traveled around the city, I was confronted by a society that I had never imagined. At the time, the caste system was still very much a part of Indian culture. Beggars were scattered along the city streets, in ragged clothing and sometimes blind. Mothers with small children, often with what appeared to be birth defects or, as was suggested, defects which had been administered in order to invoke sympathy, begged for rupees. Long horned cattle roamed the streets, often stopping traffic, which patiently waited for the animal to move. When the animals didn't, honking horns added to the chaotic scene. Traffic was horrendous and was compounded by horse carts and manned rickshaws. Along bridges and underpasses, the poor had constructed living arrangements comprised of tin, bamboo, old clothing and anything that would shelter them from the elements. In these most primitive conditions, Hindu, Muslim, Christian, Coptic, and nonreligious people were existing in extreme circumstances in India's capital city.

From New Delhi, we traveled to Hyderabad, in the central part of the country, which featured low mountain ranges, forests, which was quite rural. Four representatives from several agricultural cooperatives greeted us at the airport and drove us about fifty miles into the countryside. India experiences a monsoon season every year; sometimes as much as one hundred inches of rain over several weeks can be quite common. Therefore, there was a keen interest in mushroom farming because mushrooms required a shady, moist climate. By this time, it was late afternoon, and we pulled up in front of a cinder block building with a burlap cover over the front entrance, and similar covers over the four openings on each side of the building. This was to be our motel for the night! There was no running water, no toilet facilities, and of course, no electricity! Our hosts had brought food for dinner and breakfast the next day, and gallon jugs of water; we would cook by an open fire. A small latrine was dug several yards from the building to take care of our bodily functions. Flashlights were made available, and mosquito netting was required to cover the straw mats we were provided for sleeping, for this was the forest primeval! We were not being tested! This was "living" in rural India. Our coop friends, knowing that we had a travel schedule to maintain, wanted to show us, the next day, those ideal conditions for growing mushrooms.

March, 1992
India

As we retired for the night, two of the four of our coop friends went to the van and took out two rifles! They indicated that they would stand guard on either side of the building because of the danger of tigers in the forest! They would guard in shifts, so that there would be two people alert at all times during the night. Just about the time they finished their comments, we heard a distant roar and growling from the forest, perfect timing with their explanation! With our plane and overland travel, our camping out and the fresh air, Sultan and I both slept very well, and awoke to the aroma of fresh coffee. After breakfast, we traveled to an open air, thatched roof pavilion, where we met other members of several cooperatives and we discussed their interest in agriculture and especially mushroom farming. They explained that they needed funding to begin their operation, but more than funding, they need a business plan, and a "thinking through" process which Sultan and I initiated. At the end of the day, we left with the promise that we would investigate possible funding sources with USAID and other agencies, but we stressed that they required some intense planning in order to qualify for any development assistance. This was one of those experiences which needed the Indian government's help, which would, on the short run, not be forthcoming. We departed from the cooperative site, knowing at least we had initiated a thought process that would lend itself to a more positive outcome at a later time.

We flew from Hyderabad to Madras, which was a much larger city, and was officially known as Chennai. It was the capital of the Tami Nadu state and was located in the southeastern part of India on the Bay of Bengal. It was known as the first British outpost in India and the East India Trading Company was prominent in its development. We went there because of the interest of one of NCBA's members in importing tires from India to sell to consumer cooperatives in the United States. Dr. Sharma had made an appointment for us with the Vice President of Operations at the Tata plant, who arranged for a tour of the tire making manufacturing facility. He explained that the specifications for their tires had been provided by a consultant from the US, who had worked in one of the major manufacturing facilities there. After the tour, we discussed the request of the NCBA member who was interested in establishing a relationship with Tata. He indicated that he would be very interested in such an opportunity, *but* he was not optimistic! He indicated that the trading relationship between India and the US was not a reliable one. India still maintained tariffs and taxes on exported goods, and even imported goods. Also, the tire manufacturing unions in the United States had periodically lobbied against importing tires, not only from India, but from other countries. Sultan and I had received a lesson in international trade and politics from a very knowledgeable Indian officer who really would have liked to sell tires in the US. We left Madras on a Friday afternoon, with the prospect of meeting Sultan's wife's parents in Dhaka, the capital of Bangladesh. In addition, Bangladesh, at the time, provided clothing, and other consumer goods sold by cooperatives in the United States. As we discovered, many women were employed in this process, often supporting their families, even with their meager incomes, in less than ideal working conditions.

March, 1992
India-Bangladesh
Sultan and I stayed at a small hotel at the edge of the city which catered to international tourists. As we exited from the taxi, I noticed an eight foot wall around the hotel, and, on top of the wall was another high set of barbed wire with tiny bells sprinkled throughout! Sultan explained that the precautions were designed for the protection of guests due to periodic outbursts of civil unrest. Bangladesh is one of the world's poorest nations, which was spun-off from Pakistan after the partition of India and Pakistan in the late 1940's. It has one of the most dense populations of most countries in the world; about 2100 people per square mile, and has a hot humid climate, receiving about 80-90 inches of rain each year. Like India, it is dry in the Winter, but, subject to monsoon rains and cyclones in the Summer. The flooding during the Summer season, often claims hundreds, and sometimes several thousand victims. It has an agricultural economy which allows for little export opportunities-the people need the food which they grow and harvest. It is a much poorer country than even the poorest of the poor which I witnessed in India!

Ramadan, the ninth month of the Muslim year, had recently begun, which requires that those of the Muslim faith must fast during the daylight hours. There were a few exceptions, such as the sick or the military, but the fasting requirement was strictly adhered to for most Muslims. Because Ramadan follows the lunar calendar, Ramadan falls in different seasons. The first revelation of the Koran, revealed by God to Muhammad, was in the ninth month of the lunar calendar, and hence, the significance of Ramadan.

We went from the hotel to Sultan's wife's (Farida) parents, in the center of the city, and arrived just as the sun was setting. They had invited several aunts and uncles and it was a festive evening. They had a spacious apartment which included several bedrooms, a sitting room, a dining area, and a small kitchen. The first thing I noticed was the aroma of different spices all blended together, most of which, as I came to learn, I had never heard of! Farida's parents were involved in several businesses, one of which was the manufacturing of clothing, exported to the United States for sale in cooperative businesses. They had prepared about ten to twelve separate tapas-like dishes, consisting of chickpeas, rice, steamed vegetables, flakey cinnamon sticks, small strips of fish, and several puddings! It was a feast, which was accompanied by several different kinds of tea. We had a lively discussion, which included local and international politics.

The next day, we took a cab into downtown Dhaka near the waterfront, which experiences terrible flooding during the monsoon season. We saw a wreck of a large fishing boat which had been taken over by squatters, and there were many, many men women and children living on that hulk. On the bank of the river, we saw people with make-shift hovels strapped together with rope, tin strips and pieces of wood. Many were cooking over fires of debris and wood. It was a scene of poverty which I'll never forget. As we tried to make our way to the main street, we were surrounded by many ragged, begging children and we were concerned that they would not let us hail a cab. We took about ten US single dollars and threw them into the air and the children ran after and fought over them, giving us time to get a taxi and lock the doors. We felt so very sorry for all those children and the poverty we had seen that morning. The taxi was able to move slowly out of the waterfront and back to our hotel. We telephoned Farida's parents and thanked them again for a wonderful evening, packed our bags and left for the airport and then back to the United States. Upon arriving in Washington, D.C., as I got off the ramp, I kissed the ground, thankful for the life that I had, yet knowing that my life could never be the same, after witnessing the poverty, and understanding the will to live and survive under very primitive conditions, which I had seen in India and Bangladesh.

WEST AFRICA
Niger and Mali
1992

S eptember, 1992
Niamey, Niger

After attending the grand opening of the ACE Center in Prague, I flew initially to Paris for an overnight stay, and then the next morning I was booked on Air Afrique to Niger. Air Afrique, at that time, was regarded as safe, but not reliable when it came to adhering to a regular schedule, as I discovered later in my travels in Africa! Niger was located in the Sahel, which was in the lower section of the Sahara Desert; it was hot, and in September, very hot. Jim Alrutz, Vice President of CLUSA-Africa, had arranged this fact-finding trip for me, in order to gain a first-hand view of cooperative work in the central portion of the continent. Our man on the ground, Papa Sene, was a native of Senegal, spoke French and a number of local dialects, and was a key figure in our continuing work in Niger. Papa was a force for change in an area where change came very slowly, and had discovered that the cooperative model, especially in the engagement of people in gaining education and then reaping the rewards of their labor for themselves and their families, was an important element in accepting change in the manner of doing business. At that time, Papa Sene was in Mali, which was my next stop after a scheduled visit to a number of coops in Niger. Therefore, I was met at the airport by Lyle Brenneman, a consultant who had worked in Africa for a number of years on CLUSA Projects. Lyle indicated that we would be staying at a small hotel on the outskirts of Niamey, the capital, near one of the bends of the Niger River, which is spanned by the Kennedy Bridge, named after the US President, John F. Kennedy, who had visited Niger thirty years earlier.

As we drove to the hotel, Lyle briefly reviewed the history of Niger, and our work there. It was a country of about four hundred and eighty thousand square miles and was extremely arid with a population of thirteen million who were 80 percent Muslim, most of whom were engaged in some form of agriculture, primarily to feed themselves and their families. There were two indigenous groups, the Fulani and the Tuareg, who were nomadic and raised cattle and goats and were not engaged in agriculture. The crops that were generally grown were millet, sorghum, cassava, cotton, and of course, chickens and goats for protein. Our projects in Niger had focused on assisting coops with "dry-farming" methods because of the arid conditions, which had prevailed for years. Water, therefore, was a very precious commodity, and well-digging and irrigation were part and parcel of any agricultural endeavor. Papa Sene had worked through French-speaking "*assistants*" whom he hired from the French bureaucracy in the region and unfortunately, they had not exhibited the same concern for change that Papa Sene was trying to instill in Niger. Therefore, our projects were in a transitional period, which, in many ways was an ideal time to be there.

Another challenge for the project leaders was the reality that many of the tribal chiefs and most of the villagers could not read or write! Many could speak French, and their local dialects, but few had any years of formal education. A critical skill in the application of the dry farming techniques was the ability to read labels attached to bags of seeds, fertilizers, calculations of water amounts, etc. As Lyle pointed out, "We had to step back, in order to go forward!" Therefore, in each village, we had to set up a training class in basic reading and writing skills, as well as arithmetic training, in order to grow and process any agricultural output. As we made our way to the hotel, I became more aware of the challenges of working in Niger. We arrived at the hotel at dusk, and found that the restaurant was an open-air large thatched rectangle, with tables surrounding a fiery barbecue pit, with a grate where the chef was cooking skewers of chicken and goat meat. The taste and the aroma were terrific! Our accommodations were much like the restaurant; that is, small thatched roof huts, accommodating one person with a wooden door and bamboo-like walls, with one electric light bulb and lots of mosquito netting! The bathroom was a latrine which could be accessed with a walk outside! These were standard accommodations for working in Africa.

September, 1992
Niamey, Niger

After a great night's sleep, we had breakfast under the thatched rectangle, and Lyle warned me that the temperature could climb to one hundred and twenty degrees in the sun, so hats and several gallons of water for each of us had to be prime requisites for our travel for the day. We would be visiting a village where an open air large concrete block building had been erected where classes of reading and writing French were being led by one of the assistants. The classes were held in the early morning before the heat of the day, and the opportunity for some breeze through the openings in the sides of the building were possible. Before approaching the classroom, we had to pay our respects to the Chief of the village, and his entourage, which was absolute protocol in every village, as I learned. I had worn long pants, and a long-sleeved shirt, as well as a cap to heed Lyle's warning to avoid sunstroke. The chief came forward from his hut to meet us and he was dressed in long flowing, brightly colored robes, a beautifully embroidered skull cap, and several gold necklaces. Several of his wives were with him. Then panic struck! I had brought a compass, and a wrist watch to give to him as gifts, which was also expected, and I had left them at the hotel! Then, I remembered that when we came from the airport the previous night, I had left the two travel kits, which Air France, and Air Afrique had given me, which was the custom for airlines to give to travelers at that time, in our vehicle. I ran back to where we had parked, retrieved the kits, and brought them to the chief, who wasn't quite certain what they were, but was pleased! We could now proceed with our mission. The village consisted of a cluster of thatched roof huts, with dirt floors mostly covered with mats for sleeping, and chickens and goats scattered here and there among the huts. Some children were playing with rag balls and sticks, and a group of women were preparing food over an open fire.

The cinder block building had been erected next to a tree about fifteen feet tall which provided some shade, and was the only tree within sight. Most of the trees had been cut down for firewood which added to the arid feeling in the village. There were about twelve students, all young men, inside the building and had been selected based upon their curiosity, their commitment to learning and their interest in helping their village. The women, traditionally, raised the children, prepared the meals, and as I discovered, were in charge of finding water in their spare time. They used a divining rod which was a slingshot looking piece of wood with an extended handle, and we were told that they were quite adept at their task, because water was so critical to the survival of the village. The lessons were taught in French, and a large blackboard was used for instruction. Students were asked to come to the blackboard and answer questions and write their answers on the board. There were no notebooks or pens or pencils, but there were handouts for the students to keep and study from for the next lesson. Classes were held about every other day, for the students also had work to do in the village. Their education was a commitment by them and by the village to learn the techniques of dry farming. Essentially, this type of farming was designed to use specialized seeds, unique fertilizers and minimal irrigation to achieve success. Therefore, education regarding the purchase, and application of these elements was critical!

September, 1992
Niamey, Niger

The class continued for several hours, then, we all took a break for tea. It was served by one of the village women, who had been preparing it over an open fire, and she ladled the strong, black tea into small glasses. As I discovered in Africa, the tea was always dark and hearty, and during my travels, my teeth were stained a dark tan! I wasn't certain that I would ever get them white. After the break, the class continued until early afternoon, and then, because of the severe heat, we finished at that time, for the day. Lyle and I then traveled back to the city, and went to the project office to meet the administrative staff, who were mainly natives, along with two Caucasians. They all spoke French, and several spoke English and the native dialect, and gave the impression that they were committed to assisting in the success of the project; they were organized, and an air of competency prevailed. Later, in my travels in Mali, Papa Sene indicated that he hoped that the teacher-assistants in the field in Niger would reach the same level of commitment as the administrative staff. He finally had to make several personnel changes in the teaching staff which improved the results of the students in a dramatic fashion. Lyle spoke French and I could understand some of the teaching dialogue, but I was much better at listening than speaking! The reverse could be said of several of the teachers in Niger.

The project in Niger was cofounded by USAID and the equivalent government agency in France, which was a unique approach to development. It was gratifying to learn that the two countries were working together to provide assistance where it was really needed, but the teacher-assistants had come recommended through the French agency, and several, unfortunately, retained a bureaucratic approach evident in some government employees throughout the world. Papa Sene was attempting to introduce a gradual change in attitude and approach by the students and therefore, he had to maintain a delicate balance; on one hand retaining the funding from the French agency, and on the other, striving for an innovative education approach, which would yield results for the students. In my view, his balancing act was working and would get even better. Our travels to several other villages under the auspices of the project continued throughout the week, with the emphasis on reading and writing in order to understand the requirements for planting, irrigation, and the concept of dry-farming. All of these villages were within thirty to forty miles of Niamey. As we met the chief of each village, we remembered to bring gifts, which included fruit, vegetables, flowers etc. to recognize his status.

The day before I was to travel to Mali, we checked in with the project office and were told that the chief of the village, with whom we had visited the first day of my stay in Niger, wanted to talk with us, so Lyle and I drove out to see him in mid-morning. The chief greeted us with enthusiasm, and bear hugs! The travel kits which we had given him contained soap, cologne, tooth paste, shavers and lotion, etc. which he had been using. The women in the village, in addition to his wives, were following him around, encouraged by the new look and aroma of the chief! He was more popular than ever before. To show his appreciation, he brought out a live guinea hen and five dozen eggs from various sources (of course, in 120 degree heat)! We bowed and thanked him, glad that our gifts from the first day had made such an impression. We took the guinea hen and eggs back to the office where we distributed the eggs to staff; Holly, an Australian staffer, took the guinea hen and said she would cook a farewell dinner for Lyle and me that evening. We went to her small apartment, where she served the hen with rice and vegetables, and a cool local wine. She did her best, but we agreed that it was the toughest chicken we had ever tried to eat, and settled for a vegetarian dinner, one that I would never forget. The next morning, I flew Air Afrique to Bamako, Mali.

September, 1992
Bamako, Mali

Bamako is the capital of Mali; I arrived in the early evening, and it was as warm as Niger at that time of day. Lyle Brenneman had returned to Washington, D.C., so I had made arrangements to connect with Jeff Felton, Project Manager of the project in Mali. Jeff met me in the baggage claim area (although I had just a small suitcase), and took me to his cozy rental home to meet his wife Cheri and their ten month old son. Their home was just outside the city, and Cheri had fixed a light supper of salad, rolls, and lemonade—just perfect. I stayed with them the first night, and as opposed to Niger, there were walls in the house, no thatched roof, and a widow air conditioner—I was really living! The ever-faithful mosquito netting was a prerequisite, however, in that, malaria was a continuing problem in West Africa. I should mention that in all of my travels in some remote, strange and mysterious places, I never became ill or missed a day of work! The injections and tablets from the staff at Travel Center at American University were "on the mark" and I'll forever be thankful for their expertise. After a breakfast of croissants and coffee, Jeff and I went to the project office to meet the administrative staff and get briefed on the week ahead. Jeff was a very organized individual and produced a map of the area where each of the educational centers were, and our travel schedule for the period ahead. As in Niger, it was necessary to take a step back; that is, to focus on reading and writing skills for the students to insure their grasp of the dry farming techniques.

The office staff was very welcoming and indicated that I was the first NCBA/CLUSA officer to review the project in Mali and that they were honored that I had taken the time to be with them. I explained that I had a responsibility to review their progress and report back to USAID, but I appreciated their welcome. The staff were all from Mali, and Jeff and I were the only Caucasians there, but it was evident to me that because Jeff had married an African lady; he had a special place of respect and admiration from the staff. I met Papa Sene briefly before he had to travel to his home in Senegal, but he indicated that I would experience a much different, much more positive impression during my visit in Mali, as compared to Niger, and, he was absolutely correct. Again, at our first stop at a village about thirty-plus miles outside the city center, I brought the compass that I had intended to give to the chief in Niger, to the chief in Mali, and he was delighted.

Mali was the largest country in West Africa, about five hundred thousand square miles with a population of about fifteen million. It was bordered on the north by Algeria, on the east and southeast by Niger, on the south by Burkina Faso, and Cote d'Ivoire, and on the west by Guinea, Senegal, and Mauritania. It was a more prosperous country than Niger, and exported cotton, livestock, and fish. The area near the Niger and Senegal Rivers was the most fertile, but most of the country was semi-desert and was part of the Sahel, the southern portion of the Sahara Desert. The Fulani and the Tuareg were the primary indigenous, nomadic people, and the latter were known as the "blue people" because of their clothing *and*, the blue dye which they use to decorate their bodies, especially their faces. They were known as fierce fighters!

These two indigenous groups were not part of our project, but they were fascinating, as I learned more about each of them. They were not farmers, but raised sheep and cattle, rode horses and camels, and lived in tents. Their culture was closer to that of the Arabs and other tribes of the desert. They knew where the oases were to water their herds, and sold their livestock and the crafts and jewelry which they made in order to barter and/or buy feed for their animals. They were constantly on the move and didn't pay much attention to government or what might be considered the benefits of civilization. They made beautiful saddles for their horses and camels, which were decorated with silver and gold. They covered their faces, and usually wore turbans and long flowing gowns, not only to keep out of the blazing sun, but to ward off evil spirits. They did not like their pictures taken, although I once was able to convince a young man to do so if I offered him money. The men (although I never saw an indigenous woman or girl) wore medal medallions on the outside of their vests, which often included crosses embedded within male and female icons. I bought several of these medallions and brought them home for my wife, Ellen, and daughters, Beth and Susan.

September, 1992
Bamako, Mali

The assistant-teachers in Mali had not been selected from the French bureaucracy, yet most had some form of teaching experience, which was immediately evident. They were motivated and their enthusiasm was contagious to the students and, I must say, to Jeff and to me! Similar to our experience in Niger, our travels throughout the week took us to villages with outdoor thatched rectangular structures, equipped with benches and a blackboard. The students from each one of these villages where the projects had been identified had been selected based upon their interest and their expressed desire to assist their respective villages. Each time we took a break with the students, they were interested in where I was from, the kind of classrooms we had in the United States, and if the classes were held outside! They spoke in French, and although I could understand some of their questions, Jeff was an excellent interpreter. Also, we were always offered a small glass of hot, black tea and I began to understand that hot tea was the drink of choice morning, noon, and night. Because there was no refrigeration in the villages, ice tea in the prevailing heat would have been very much appreciated, but not available. Yet, the hot tea seemed to keep one's mind off the heat all around us, and I began not to be bothered as much about the high temperatures. In addition, scalding water killed most of the germs and I never had a digestive problem.

Because of the early success of the teaching and learning in Mali, Jeff and I were invited to the equivalent of a high school graduation ceremony, which was not connected to our projects, but because of our involvement in Mali, we were invited to attend. The ceremony was held about fifty miles outside the city, and again, in a very large open area. Fortunately, trees circled the commencement, so there was some shade for the crowd. We had to park our truck about a mile from the ceremony because we discovered that there would be about five hundred graduates from several schools, and a similar number of family members and guests. We were the only Caucasians. Also, several government dignitaries were on the dais to present the diplomas to the graduates, both male and female, whose names were called, not in French, but in the local dialect. Then, male African dancers, dressed in bright feathers, and beads, with colorful sashes and loin cloths, accompanied by drums and flutes, honored the graduates with a traditional presentation of chanting and leaping which would have resembled the best in ballet, anywhere! It was announced that a buffet would be served for everyone, and because we were guests, we followed the government dignitaries to the large tent which shielded tables from the sun filled with fruit, vegetables and chicken and goat. It was magnificent!

Because of the huge crowd, we finished our food before everyone had been fed, but then, an additional part of the ceremony began. A handsome, six and a half foot Malian, dressed in embroidered yellow gown which stretched the length of his frame, topped by a matching yellow cap, began circulating among the guests carrying a large woven basket. He was the interlocutor; that is, the town crier of the villages. He was collecting money to help defray expenses for the ceremony and especially for the buffet. Jeff and I had left our wallets in the truck, and we looked at one another with panic, in that, it was too far to retrieve our cash. He finally made his way to where we were sitting and held out the basket. I stood up with my hands open and then remembered that I had a brand new Schaefer silver pen and pencil set in my shirt pocket, which had been given to me before I came to Africa. I approached him and held out the set. He did not put them in the basket, but held them up for all to see, and then began to weep! The crowd became completely silent, and I thought I had committed a terrible faux pas. All of a sudden, the crowd began to cheer, and applaud, and several of the teachers came and took each of his arms and led him away. The buffet was finally finished, and the crowd was beginning to talk informally, and a reporter from Bamako came up to Jeff and me and explained what had happened. We had given the perfect gift and although it wasn't money, it was much better and that's why the crowd reacted the way it did and was the reason he started to cry. Our gift of the silver pen and pencil set was a challenge to him and to the crowd that he, just like the students who learned how to read and write, must learn those skills! Because he could do neither! A number of the parents and guests came up to us after the ceremony, expressing their appreciation for our attending the ceremony and for giving this honored interlocutor this special gift. As Jeff and I made our way back to the truck, the sun was beginning to set, and we confirmed what a great experience it was, and that we would forever be thankful to the Schaefer Company for their beautiful writing set!

I was scheduled to return to the US the next day, Thursday, because the following week, interviews for the Presidency of NCBA, CLUSA, and CBI were scheduled to begin on Monday morning. I didn't know when my interview was scheduled, but I knew that it would be early in the week and I wanted to be as fresh as possible. I was scheduled to fly Air Afrique early the next morning to Paris, then on to Washington, D.C. However, Air Afrique did not leave the next day, and finally, late in the afternoon on Saturday, I was on my way to Paris. United Airlines put me up in a room at the airport after noting my schedule was fouled up. I was up early and went to the customer service desk where the agent told me that there was a conference of economists in Washington and that there were no seats available! She gave me the best advice from an agent that I ever received. She said, "Mr. Notar, there may be standby's available. It's doubtful, but possible. Get to the gate as early as you can and tell the gate agent you are flying on operator #13 status." I asked what that was, and she indicated, "Just do it!" I did as she commanded and found that there were five standby seats available. I was awarded the 5th standby seat which happened to be in first class (on an economy ticket). Although I did not look or smell like a first class passenger, I enjoyed the perks of the moment.

I finally arrived at Dulles Airport in Washington, D.C. on Sunday evening and collected my one bag and was processed by the customs agent. He asked, "Are you DOD?" I said no. Again, he asked, "Are you CIA?" I replied that I wasn't! Finally, he said that if I was part of the

Defense Department, or the Central Intelligence Agency, I couldn't tell him anyhow! He apologized for asking! The agent at United Airlines had provided the highest security rating that she could and it was enough to get me on the plane and back to D.C.! I did get to my office on Monday morning, somewhat worse for wear and tear, to find that my interview was scheduled for 10:00 A.M. As they say, the rest is history; after several interviews and meetings with the NCBA Board of Directors, I was awarded the job. It was the beginning of several significant challenges during my tenure, but none of it would probably have been possible without the agent from United Airlines!

BRAZIL
1993

1 993
Ohio Farm Bureau Fact Finding Trip
Brazil

Shortly after I was elected President and CEO of NCBA and CBI in February, 1993, I was invited to accompany a delegation of the Ohio Farm Bureau to travel to the Parana Region of Brazil. This region was known as the "terra roxa" (for purple soil) of the Parana in Southwest Brazil, because of its long growing season and its ideal climate for agricultural products, especially soybeans, corn and alfalfa. Included in the delegation were Bill and Helen Swank (Bill was Executive Director of the Ohio Farm Bureau), Dave and Theresa Miller (Dave was a Director of the Farm Bureau and a Director of the Nationwide Insurance Company, and a member of the NCBA Board) and other Nationwide directors including Henry and Barbara Holloway, and Bob and Gwen Stewart.

The delegation flew into Sao Paulo, the largest city in Brazil (about twenty-plus million at the time) and met with the United States Embassy staff to obtain a briefing on the current state of events—particularly agricultural problems and achievements in Brazil. From the air, Sao Paulo looked like the biggest city I had ever seen, stretching out over the horizon with skyscrapers, highways, and many trucks and automobiles! Although the capital is Brasilia, Sao Paulo looked to be where the action was! Roberto Rodriguez, a farmer, trader, and cooperative businessman in Brazil, who, at the time, was the elected volunteer President of the International Cooperative Alliance, had arranged for a large van and driver to take all of us on our mission. That mission was to travel southwest from Sao Paulo to the intersection of Brazil, Argentina and Uruguay, a distance of about one thousand miles, visiting cooperatives, and collecting and exchanging information.

The next morning, we were met by Mauro Campo, a coop staff member, with a large, comfortable van and we headed into the countryside. Obviously, we would be in close contact with one another, living out of our suitcases, and staying at modest inns and hotels along the route. At the end of eight days, we would hopefully have a much better understanding of Brazilian agriculture and the cooperators who were making it their life's work. The first day, our schedule took us to a small coop farm (one to two hundred hectares) which was engaged in growing soybeans. We were told that if the highway system (primarily the use of semi-trailer trucks) in Brazil was modernized (expanded east, west, north and south), it would help farmers tremendously. In that area of Brazil, the climate was so favorable, that two separate crops of soybeans could have been harvested and sold on the world market each year. That development would have been a real competitive challenge to the US. Time and again, we were told in our travels that the lack of distribution and marketing hindered Brazilian farmers.

As we traveled throughout the Parana, we stopped at large coop farm (two to five thousand hectares) that raised cattle, soybeans and alfalfa along with chickens, pigs and goats. Several had their own processing operations, and refrigerated barns, along with huge storage facilities for their grains. We witnessed very sophisticated farming operations rivaling any that the Ohio delegation were familiar with at home. The larger farms were expecting us and often had picnic lunches laid out under tents along with soft drinks and wine. The women in our group had an opportunity to exchange information with the wives of the cooperators and discovered that, like most everywhere in the world, the entire farm family works, including grown children, to insure that the many details of a successful farm are taken care of. Mauro, our driver, sometimes had to interpret for us, but generally, most people we met spoke English. Bill Swank usually provided a description of the Ohio Farm Bureau, and the federated system of agricultural cooperatives in the United States. That is, cooperatives may have sold their products to buyers, or consolidated distributors, who in turn may have sold to overseas customers or those in the US.

We continued our trip southwestward, and on one occasion, stopped at a cooperative which was making furniture. The name Brazil had its derivation from a Portuguese word, *brasa*, which meant, glowing coal, a description given to Brazil wood which had as its properties a vibrant red color. Brazil's population was diverse in that it contained Portuguese, Spanish, Guarni Indians (depicted in the modern film, *The Mission*) and former slaves, pirates, etc. The state language was Portuguese, but we also discovered that a small portion of the population was Japanese. These people left Japan, many at the turn of the twentieth century for work, others after WWII. Brazil was soccer crazy and has won the World Cup, the highest achievement in soccer. Many cooperatives had photos of Pele, the greatest Brazilian player ever, according to most people. Obviously, our delegation talked about football and baseball, as we exchanged stories about our respective cultures. This particular coop had an assembly line of wood, from handling of the raw trees to the beautiful finished products of chairs, tables and accessories. We had visited about ten separate cooperatives by that time, and Dave Miller's wife, Theresa, like all the rest of us, was hot and tired. Finally, she broke the tension, by saying, "I hope that this is the last stop, I don't want to see another coop on this trip!" That got a great laugh and that was the last stop! We all had seen a significant portion of Brazil in a very short time.

Our final stop was at Iguacu Falls in Brazil, which contains twenty-seven separate waterfalls, and it was regarded as one of the world's great wonders. Eleanor Roosevelt, who visited Iguacu some years before, was quoted as saying, after viewing the tremendous display, "Poor little Niagara!" Iguacu had a Brazilian side and an Argentinean side and one could walk across a bridge to view the falls which is quite an experience. That night, we stayed at the inn on the Brazil side and had hot showers, comfortable beds, and a great meal. The Farm Bureau delegation was continuing their trip to Argentina, while I had to return to Washington, D.C. to begin my new job. My impressions of Brazil were quite positive. It was as large as the United States in land mass, and has twenty-six states, plus Brasilia, the capital. The country had vast mineral resources, good seaports, and a growing climate that rivaled any in the world. The cooperative community in Brazil was vibrant, organized and contained excellent leadership. My observations, based upon our contacts throughout the Parana state, confirmed that Brazil needed stable, visionary leadership at the top political levels in order to promote education and eliminate poverty and organize its financial leadership to compete on a sophisticated global scale. The lack of commitment to improve roads, bridges, and waterways, as noted above, continued to hinder the development of markets, at home and abroad. However, this trip was a confirmation to me of the growing importance of cooperatives as part of, not only the Brazilian economy, but offering individuals an opportunity to participate through the cooperative model, in a way that had not been available to them in the past, thereby raising living standards, and providing for educational opportunities for themselves and their children. I returned to Washington, D.C. with renewed energy and hope for the future of cooperatives.

INDONESIA
1992-1998

O ctober, 1992
Yogyakarta, Indonesia

Because my initial trip to Indonesia was interrupted by the explosion of Mt. Pinatubo in the Philippines, this time, I planned to fly directly into Jakarta, the capital city of Indonesia, on the northwestern side of the island of Java. From there, I hopped on to a commuter flight on Garuda Airlines to Yogyakarta, the ancient capital, and now a bustling university city on the southeastern side of the Island. I was picked up at the airport by one of Sam Filiaci's staff who drove through the city at 5:00 P.M. just in time for the Muslim call to worship which came from a number of mosques scattered around the city. Several of these mosques were truly works of art and architecture, and provided an impression, along with many other buildings of a generous blend of the new and the old city. It was quite impressive!

Sam Filiaci, Vice President of NCBA (the National Cooperative Business Association), and CBI (Cooperative Business International) was the driving force of building cooperatives businesses in Indonesia. His philosophy encompassed the desire to use the cooperative model to focus workers on developing businesses that would not only bring income to them, and improve their standard of living, but grow those businesses so that products and/or services could be exported for additional income and growth. In 1992, he had succeeded in doing just that.

My job was to monitor what Sam had accomplished, offer whatever additional help we could provide from the US and determine if his management approach could be replicated in other countries which could use the cooperative model. Sam was a US citizen, and had developed his interest and expertise in cooperative development as he completed his tour with the Peace Corps, some years before.

We arrived at Sam's home, which included his office which was twenty miles outside the city. It was a sprawling farm/ranch house situated on several acres of land. He had built several barns, and sheds, which housed equipment, tractors, SUV's, etc. which were necessary to the cooperative businesses. Sam had married a beautiful Indonesian woman, a daughter of a prominent family. Their marriage was one of mutual respect and compromise. They agreed that Sam would convert to the Muslim faith, and their three daughters would retain their Muslim faith, but become US Citizens. When each of their daughters were born, they were born in Hawaii. Sam's commitment to his wife and family was well known in Yogyakarta, and beyond, and he was admired and respected for it.

Sam and his wife greeted me at the front door, and invited me into their great room. They had decorated it with woven tapestries of Indonesian history, a photograph of family members, a small set of bronze gamelan discs which were used for a special type of Indonesian music, and several shadow puppets which were used in storytelling of the history and myths of the country. It was a delightful room. Furniture included a side board used for serving, made of mahogany, and a teak set of a large table and chairs. Sam explained the schedule for the week, and then showed me to their guest room, where I would be staying. I cleaned up for dinner, which then consisted of satay (chicken with spices on sticks), rice, Indonesian style with spiced gravy, lettuce salad with bananas, oranges, and nuts, lemonade, and mango teens, which were round purple fruits about the size of an apple and very sweet. All was prepared by Sam's wife, and it was a feast for a hungry traveler. Their three daughters were very quiet, and couldn't quite figure out who this strange person was who had invaded their home. I explained that I was the father of two daughters who were much older than they were and then I showed them a photo of my wife, Ellen, and our daughters, Beth and Susan. Somehow, the fact that I also was the father of daughters made me more acceptable to them. At that time, I believe their ages were eight, six, and four. Before turning in for the night, Sam showed me his office which was in the back of the house and it was outfitted with a computer, a fax machine, and several telephones. It was the operations center for cooperatives in Indonesia.

October, 1992
Yogyakarta, Indonesia

The next morning, we were up early for a light breakfast and Sam took me out to several locations where vanilla beans were being sun dried. We were about thirty miles outside the city and the landscape was filled with rolling hills and valleys, rural in feeling, and it was beginning to get very warm. Under a thatched roof open air building, many women, dressed in traditional garb—that is, head scarves, loose fitting colorful batik sarongs, and long skirts—were sorting the dried vanilla beans into various sizes. They were also watching for beans that were not acceptable for processing. They were sitting on the ground, with their legs tucked under them, and were perfectly comfortable, as they chatted and sorted. Large earthen ware jugs of water were placed next to each woman, so that they would not succumb to heat stroke. Vanilla beans looked like dark, dried pea pods and even in this early stage of processing they had a pleasant aroma. Vanilla beans were a unique product which could only be grown in a climate which was common to Indonesia—that is, hot, humid, plenty of rainfall and many sunny days. That is not to say that vanilla couldn't be grown elsewhere, but there was a reason why Indonesia's thirteen thousand-plus islands were once called the Spice Islands. Not all of these islands were inhabited, but the enormity of all these islands under the aegis of a sovereign country was daunting.

41

Vanilla is a plant of the family of orchids where the vines flourish in hot damp climates. The natural pollinating agents are bees and hummingbirds, while commercial plants can be pollinated by hand. The source of the flavor is vanillin, which crystallizes on the outside of the seed pod after a series of curing and drying processes, often outside in direct sunlight. A continuing concern is mold which requires that the vanilla beans must be harvested and dried and kept out of the rain. The purpose of the drying procedure is to insure that the hot sun has reduced the moisture content in each bean to almost zero, so that when the beans are packed and shipped for processing no mold can develop.

Sam explained that once the beans were ready for shipment, they were loaded into burlap bags and placed in containers which then were transported to ships that would take the beans to the United States. Sam had developed a trading relationship with McCormick and Company in the US and McCormick was very pleased with the quality of the beans. They would process the beans and bottle the vanilla extract for sale, not only in the US but around the world. Of course, the cooperators whom Sam had trained, were the beneficiaries of the proceeds resulting from their labor.

Sam Filiaci's background was unique to this endeavor. He began in the Peace Corps in Africa (as many cooperative overseas managers have Peace Corps experience), and wanted to continue his overseas experience in some manner. He discovered that USAID was developing requests for proposals in developing countries, and Indonesia was among them. He was vetted by NCBA/CLUSA and was assigned to Indonesia. The initial project called for the development of a rice cooperative, but the Chinese, as Sam discovered, had that market sewed up. About that time, a terrible hurricane destroyed the vanilla crop in Madagascar and Sam, being a resourceful individual, researched the prospects for vanilla in Indonesia. He proposed the change to USAID which was approved, and his ingenuity propelled the vanilla bean cooperatives into existence. It was a true cooperative success story.

October, 1992
Yogyakarta, Indonesia

The development of cooperatives in Indonesia, as in most places, was a "bottoms up" endeavor. That is, the sale of vanilla beans provided earnings, after expenses, to the cooperative, which in turn, shared those proceeds with the coop members. The members allocated a portion of those proceeds to the new crop, and then had income of their own to provide for food, clothing and shelter for themselves and their families. One very important concern of the cooperative members was the education of their children. At that time, the state and federal allocation of funds toward education were not adequate. The history of Indonesia, both in the 19th and 20th centuries, was one of exploitation of the population. As most local people knew, one of the reasons why there was little or no upward mobility, was the lack of education. The coop members, with the emphasis that Sam Filiaci placed on the rewards the community could reap with the sharing model he introduced, was a dramatic and welcome change from the experience of their past generations. They trusted Sam, and witnessed the success of their labor! They were being educated in this business, and could visualize more formal education for their children, in the future.

The next day, Sam took me to two new ventures which were not part of the vanilla bean projects, but were constructed on the cooperative model. These new ventures included two separate wood processing operations. The first, under a large tin-roofed warehouse, open at each end, took large teak trees, which had been harvested and trimmed, and manufactured casual tables, chairs, salad bowels, and an assortment of wood accessories for the leisure markets, primarily in the United States and Europe. The second operation processed mahogany trees which were turned into much higher-end products, such as dining room tables and chairs, serving tables, and bedroom night tables. I was amazed at the craftsmanship and beautiful design of these products. Sam indicated that he had brought in "experts" to train the Indonesian craftsmen, who had quickly applied their substantial skills to the operation. The climate in Central Java was comparable in latitude to that of the mid-southeast coast of Africa, as well as the mid-southwest coast of South America. The climate conditions resulting from this geographic similarity reflected hot, moist, humid weather patterns, which were conducive to fast growing trees and shrubs. Naturally, with wood working operations, the need for safety was paramount. The workers in each of these operations wore safety goggles, gloves and long sleeved shirts, even with the hot working conditions. Fans with suction devices kept the air relatively free of sawdust, but it was hard work.

These manufacturing operations required the packing and boxing of the finished products, and the scheduling of semi-trailer trucks to take the products to transit points for shipping. All of this process was handled by the Indonesian cooperative organization. However, in any wood-based manufacturing operation, there were always splinters, cuts, and more severe accidents. Therefore, the coop built a small structure of several rooms for treating the workers. Initially, a nurse came several times a week to treat patients. Then, several of the families of workers came, with children who needed attention, and the coop hired a doctor to come several times a week. Eventually, a doctor and several nurses were hired, not only to attend to the workers' needs, but the needs of the cooperative community which the work force represented! It truly was the cooperative model at work, serving the whole community! What a thrill to see how this process evolved and the continued success which it generated.

CAPITALIZATION OF COOPERATIVE BUSINESS INTERNATIONAL (CBI)1996-1997

Background
The NCBA/CLUSA projects in Indonesia had evolved from a USAID funded series of projects, which were part of an initiative by the United States government to engage developing countries into starting business enterprises, into a full-blown series of cooperative businesses of agricultural and furniture projects managed by Sam Filiaci. Sam was an astute businessman, but he needed assistance from Cooperative Business International, (CBI), which had been formed in 1985 as a for-profit subsidiary of NCBA/CLUSA to market products from projects such as the ones in Indonesia. With his Indonesian and US contacts, projects which Sam had managed had become successful not-for-profit businesses, and needed markets! Indonesian Coop members were earning wages, as designated by their charters, and vanilla beans, coffee, spices, furniture, etc. were being sold in various quantities, the earnings of which were being returned to the various enterprises and shared by the coop members. Unfortunately, CBI had never been capitalized—no stock had been sold—so that CBI was being funded by the cooperative members' dues from NCBA. Therefore, Sam wasn't receiving much help and support from the entity that had been developed to assist him in just this kind of situation!

I was elected President of NCBA/CLUSA and CBI in 1993, and as mentioned earlier, I had traveled to Indonesia several times as an officer of NCBA, but not as President. I recognized in my earlier travels there, that Sam required capital for growth and expansion of the business enterprises there. One of my primary objectives then, as President, was to provide capital to CBI! In effect, what I wanted to do was separate the for-profit subsidiary from the not-for-profit membership association, so that CBI could stand on its own, and accomplish what it was originally intended to do! I contacted the Securities and Exchange Commission and learned that this was to be an unusual financial process, which required the development of a stock offering to be sold, not on the open market, but to NCBA members. In effect, we wanted to offer stock to a closed investor group. After that discussion, I hired a financial consultant and an attorney, Ralph K. Morris, who had been engaged in complicated cooperative issues and we went to work.

After a number of months, we had resolved several critical issues, including approval from the NCBA/ CLUSA Board of Directors to proceed. At that time, the NCBA Board also handled CBI issues. It was agreed that the stock offering to NCBA members would be in the range of one to one and a half million dollars. That amount was recommended as a realistic stock offering to be purchased by the membership. Also, it should be noted, that many members were skeptical, based upon the limited track record of CBI, that their investment would be worthwhile! In one encounter with the Chief Financial Officer of one of NCBA's key members, he indicated that he understood the objective, but he was responsible for protecting his company's assets, and its financial well-being, and he was concerned about this investment. It was that meeting which caused me to change my strategy, and I began making appointments with the presidents of our member organizations, including Nationwide Insurance Company. I met with Dimon McPherson, Nationwide's President and CEO and explained that if this stock offering was not successful, both NCBA and CBI were at risk. He agreed, and directed his staff to commit to the project!

July, 1997
Jakarta, Indonesia

The revised legal documents which had been prepared for CBI, required that a President and CEO be elected by the CBI Board of Directors, separate from the NCBA/CLUSA President and CEO (namely yours truly), so that a permanent separation would exist between the organizations. Robert Clark, from Columbus, Ohio, was elected to that office, and was known to the CBI shareholders. The CBI Board of Directors was elected from the NCBA membership, with the majority being new CBI shareholders. Don Benschneider, a successful farmer from Ohio was elected Chairman of CBI. Other required officers were elected by the CBI Board. A public accounting firm was hired to audit and confirm the financial proceedings of CBI, and it became a bonafide operating corporation, separate from NCBA. Between 1996, and mid-year 1997, we had accomplished what many thought was nearly an impossible task!

It was, therefore, a very upbeat and positive CBI Board which journeyed to Indonesia in July, 1997. Not all the board members could make the trip, but those who attended wanted to meet Sam Filiaci, and observe his successful operations there. In summary, Bob Clark, the new president, led his initial meeting overseas, and the board members had a very positive impression of the prospects for CBI as a result of these meetings. The board members returned home, but I had been asked to be one of the principal speakers to celebrate the 50th anniversary of the inception of cooperatives in Indonesia. The celebration was titled, *the Network Conference of Asia Pacific Cooperatives and Small and Medium Enterprises, July 14-15, 1997.* The Conference was held at the largest Conference Center in Jakarta, and about two thousand people attended. Representatives from China, Japan, Burma, the Philippines, Australia, etc. were there to exchange ideas and, to honor Indonesia on this significant anniversary. My remarks focused on the current trends in cooperative development in the United States in the last ten years, and included an overhead presentation which was well received. I also paid tribute to the Indonesian cooperative initiatives, and then introduced Sam Filiaci and Bob Clark, who were in the audience. That gave me an opportunity to briefly discuss the marketing opportunities which would be available to Indonesia through CBI.

After my presentation, I was invited to meet with President Suharto of Indonesia, and several others on the program, for discussion and tea and cakes during the morning break. He wore the traditional black, Muslim hat, and was dressed in a dark business suit, with a white shirt and red tie. He thanked us for our participation, and presented each of us with an eight by ten inch plaque, the top two thirds of which was in stone depicting one of the reliefs at Borobudur, the ancient Muslim temple complex near Yogyakarta. Quite a treasure! He asked if each of us had established a booth at the conference center, which was open all week, and he indicated that he would look forward to seeing our displays as he toured the center. The center was huge; I estimated that it was the size of a football field, and displayed the flags of all the countries which had participated, each of which contained the primary products and services produced by cooperatives offered by that country. Sam had set up the booth in the third aisle, about two hundred and fifty yards from the entrance to the center, which displayed vanilla beans, coffee, and furniture. Sam and I were scheduled to work with several of Sam's foremen, to staff the booth and answer questions for the rest of the week. Sam had purchased a cotton batik Indonesian shirt, in black and green tones for me, designed much as a Mexican Guayabera; Sam reasoned it would look more like I belonged there rather than a typical Arrow shirt—he was right!

The next morning, Sam and I were drinking coffee at the entrance to the center, when President Suharto arrived with his entourage. He greeted us, and asked to see our booth. Sam led the way to the third aisle and the President was pleased with the products displayed, but not with the location of the booth! He turned to one of his staff and said, "Pack up this booth and take it to the first row, near the entrance. I want everyone to see what Sam has accomplished with his American friends, here in Indonesia!" For the remainder of the week, we had a prime location for the booth which Sam and his staff had developed! Sam commented that it was all because he had purchased the Indonesian batik shirt for me! My impressions, at the end of the week, included the following:

- The Suharto regime had come to power with the overthrow of the Sukarno dictatorship in 1965, which was depicted in the 1983 film, *The Year of Living Dangerously*, directed by Peter Weir. Thousands were killed, and although conditions had improved dramatically for some the people, it was still a dictatorship.
- Jakarta was a huge, bustling city, with a population of ten million and was filled with motor bikes, bicycles, horse drawn wagons, three-wheeled taxis, and people hurrying, which was the operational word. Indonesian people, whom I met and observed, were among the hardest working, indomitable of spirit, persevering and generally positive in their outlook from many people I had encountered in my journeys. I was impressed with their intelligence and their ability to master any task in record time.

Indonesia was filled with anomalies; that is, it was not like most places in which I have worked or traveled. It was a mysterious country, and it was a country of thirteen thousand-plus islands. One of the art forms was a presentation of shadow puppets which often was accompanied by a group of musicians playing gongs, xylophones, and drums described as a gamelan. The shadow puppets were thin reed-like, beautifully decorated incarnations of Gods and Goddesses which were woven into a story of war and peace, of love and hate, of evil spirits, etc. with presentations sometimes lasting hours. It was a country of beautiful clothing, and exotic foods, and market places which were filled with birds, parrots, sculptures, and furniture!

- Indonesia had beautiful beaches, scenic mountains, volcanoes, and on some islands, and terrible poverty. One could only imagine how difficult it might have been to try to administer to a population spread over thousands of islands. Not all the islands were populated, but still, for those living in small villages or on outlying islands, they had to be of independent spirit, because there was no, or little governmental presence.

- I had the privilege of working with Sam Filiaci for several years, and he was one of the most successful, cooperative entrepreneurs that I have ever met. He has raised a family, created a number of successful cooperative enterprises and brought dignity and pride to thousands of Indonesians who have worked and prospered utilizing the cooperative model. His legacy will live for a long, long time!

January, 1998
East Timor, Indonesia

My wife, Ellen, and I flew into Jakarta, the capital city of Indonesia, then took a commuter flight on to the island of Bali, known for its Hindu population, many of whom are very talented artists and wood carvers. We stayed at the Hotel Bali Oberoi, a very nice hotel near the beach, and more importantly, very safe. The next day, early in the morning, I left Ellen, and took a flight on Garuda Airlines to the capital city of East Timor, Dili. I was scheduled to meet Sam Filiaci, Vice President of NCBA/CLUSA, who was the major contributor of his expertise, time and energy, which had made the projects in Indonesia so successful! I boarded the small plane and noticed, immediately, that I was the only civilian on board. All the passengers were in military uniforms! That observation was unnerving, but later events in my trip helped me understand the reason for the large military presence. Sam had invited me to join him in Dili, to observe several of his new projects there, including harvesting vanilla beans and coffee production. I was to report to USAID upon my return to Washington, D.C. USAID had funded these projects, not only because of Sam's highly successful track record, but also because of the simmering unrest in East Timor, a portion of which was credited to economic inequality. The island of Timor had been divided into east and west as a result of continued conflicts in the 70's and 80's between the Portuguese and the Indonesian government, and the East Timorese believed that their government was not paying attention to their need for education and economic mobility.

My arrival at the airport further confirmed my anxiety, because the military customs agent noted my small travel bag, and was concerned that I was coming to East Timor, to further incite the population against the government, which was then under the auspices of President Suharto. I assured him that my mission was not to agitate but to assist in the development of cooperatives which would be beneficial to the people and the economy. I mentioned Sam Filiaci, and that was the magic word to confirm what I had just told him. Sam and his staff were well known as individuals who had come to East Timor to help the people, not hurt the government! I finally passed through customs, and met Sam just outside the small airport. Sam explained the tension in the region as we began our visit to one of the vanilla bean projects in the white SUV which was provided by the USAID project funding.

Sam explained that Indonesia and particularly the outermost islands, such as East Timor, had a long, violent history, even before the conflicts with Portugal. The Dutch had been present in the country when the many islands were known as the Spice Islands for several hundreds of years, and at times were brutal in their treatment of the natives. Then, the Japanese invaded and had a similar brutal style to their occupation. Finally, the Australians threw the Japanese out at the end of World War II, but couldn't understand why they were not welcomed as liberators! The natives, at that point in time, didn't want to have *any* foreigners in their territory. But then, they expected some genuine assistance from their own government which was not forthcoming, at least in a timely fashion, in their minds. Therefore, there was the beginning of an independence movement in East Timor, and that was one reason why the government was interested in having the projects there, to confirm their interest in finally paying attention to the people's needs. Sam knew the risks involved, but based upon his background and experience, felt that he could really help to lend some calming influence in East Timor. As we drove, we discussed the difficulty of the Indonesian government trying to manage over thirteen thousand islands, not all of which were inhabited. East Timor had a population of over two hundred and fifty thousand, most of whom are of the Muslim faith, with a minority of Hindus. We concluded that it would be a difficult assignment for any government, and therefore concluded that we could understand the underlying tension and unrest. We stayed at a small pension in Dili for several nights and it was clean with bunk beds, and a shower. The lady in charge offered the room and breakfast, but also was concerned as to our business in East Timor. We assured her we were not on the island to cause trouble.

January, 1998
East Timor, Indonesia

After traveling to several of the projects during the week, Sam and I were ready to leave East Timor. Our plan was to fly to Bali, pick up Ellen and then fly on to Yogyakarta, where Ellen and I would spend the weekend before flying home. We planned to have dinner with Sam and his family on Saturday evening. Sam had arranged to have our tickets on Air Garuda leaving Dili on Friday afternoon, since Ellen already had her tickets. We got to the airport about 3:30 P.M. since our flight was scheduled for 4:30, and we each had small carry-on bags. All we had to do was check-in. However, the airport was in chaos, in that many of the military personnel wanted to leave East Timor to go to Jakarta for "R & R" because there wasn't much night life to be enjoyed in Dili! In addition, the military were not very welcome there, as I described earlier. The seats on the last plane for the day had been oversold, and the military felt that they had priority and were using their muscle to insure that they had all the seats! Sam went to the gate agent (not the check-in desk), whom he knew, and the agent took our tickets and said, "Run for the plane, there are two seats left," and that's what we did!

We took off running as hard as we could, and we could see the pilot revving-up the engines (it was a propeller engine plane), and the ground crew were preparing to take the stairs away from the plane's doorway. All of a sudden, we heard gunshots coming from the airport; some of the soldiers were firing at us for taking the last two seats! We never did know if they were trying to hit us or scare us, but the pilot seeing what was happening was concerned about the bullets hitting the fuselage. One of the stewardesses had apparently told him we were running to board the plane, so he hesitated long enough for us to get into the plane and he was moving before we ever got to the two remaining seats! They were not our seats and they weren't together, but we had made it! Perspiring heavily, we settled in, and some of the other passengers (not the military) applauded our running and dodging skills! We were able to pick up Ellen in Bali, and fly on to Yogyakarta, where Sam went on home and we went to a hotel in the city.

Ellen mentioned that at the hotel she was staying at in Bali, the staff could not quite comprehend why "a lady alone" was in Bali! She finally explained that her husband was working in East Timor, and they were very concerned that I would make it back to Bali to pick her up. East Timor was not a safe place to be! On Saturday, Sam arranged for us to go to two world class architectural wonders, the temples of Borobudur, and Prambanan. Borobudur was built about 800 A.D. and its name means "Buddhist monastery on the hill", and what a hill it was! It rose out of a small field and included sixty thousand cubic meters of stone, and was decorated with relief panels which included elephants, dancing girls and kings, and textbook doctrines of the Buddhist religion. It was topped by one of South-East Asia's most prominent religious relics, and ranks with Cambodia's Angkor Wat, and Burma's Pagan as magnificent wonders of a bygone era. It was huge! Prambanan was a group of Hindu temples, and was only fifty kilometers from Borobudur. It was constructed about the middle of the 9th century, and included eight major temples; the most prominent of which was the temple of Shiva, the Destroyer, a statue of which stood on a huge lotus leaf. There were also eight minor temples, which have been restored. It was estimated that there were still two hundred and forty-four smaller temples on the site which were in various stages of rehabilitation! Ellen and I marveled that two distinct religions built these huge monuments so close together, and these formidable structures survived to this present time. History suggests that the worshipers of each lived in relative harmony throughout the millennia.

We had dinner with Sam and his wife and three daughters that evening, filled with awe and admiration for this beautiful, mysterious, and historic country which we had learned to admire more and more as we had contact and discussion with the people there. We flew back home the next day filled with the hope that we could return someday and spend more time when work was not the main reason to be there!

EL SALVADOR
1994-1997

January, 1994
El Salvador
My initial working trip to El Salvador occurred just after the New Year when CO-BANK Chair, Otis Molz, and a group of NCBA Directors wanted to view and experience, first hand, the work of Stanley and Gloria Kuehn in this war torn country. Stan and Gloria had begun work, through a USAID grant to CLUSA, the international arm of NCBA, prior to the intermittent civil war, but had to return to the US because of the danger. They had now begun, again, under very difficult circumstances. Their mission was to provide technical assistance in the formation of cooperatives throughout the country, but especially in those areas which had been the most devastated by the civil war. Stan was an agricultural specialist, a graduate of Texas A&M, whose father had also been active in assisting agricultural coops in Latin America and the US. Gloria was a Latina, spoke fluent Spanish, and played an extremely important role in involving the Salvadorian women in the formation of cooperatives throughout the country.

The people of El Salvador were at the center of the "liberation theology" movement in Latin America. Bishop Romero, an intelligent, concerned priest, had witnessed the continued power of the "14 families". They were the wealthy land owners, traders and military elite whose focus was building their wealth and, at the same time, keeping the men, women and children "the peons" from sharing in that wealth. Education, medical care, home ownership, etc. were excluded from much of the population. These ruling families coordinated their hold on power with the military, and did not want *any* type of opportunity for the people, whether it be theological, economic or educational. The people's concerns, led by Bishop Romero, were labeled "communism" and drew the attention of the US which was concerned about the stability of the region, and therefore was not supportive of the liberation theology of Bishop Romero. I will expand on this issue later, but in a number of visits to El Salvador, I did not see nor experience any support of communist doctrine.

Basically, the country was being run by a right-wing group of militarists backed by a complicit government, and Bishop Romero and a group of priests implored the US to recognize the issues of oppression, lack of education for children and terrible poverty and take action to assist the people. For his activism, Bishop Romero was assassinated on March 24, 1980, as he said Mass at a church for cancer patients in San Salvador, the capital. He did not have an agenda for the country—some accused him of socialism—but he wanted to protect the people, and help them achieve a better life. In addition, several other priests and nuns disappeared, during the 1980's! Many of the men and women of El Salvador could not stand by and see their church leaders and others killed for trying to help them. So began a series of actions against the military, who were enforcing the political power of the elite. These actions during the latter part of the 1980's became a full-fledged civil war with thousands of men, women and children killed, along with thousands of military. Finally, in early 1992, peace accords were signed with sponsorship by the US and other Latin American countries, and it was then, that Stan and Gloria Kuehn returned to El Salvador, with their three children, to begin, again, to introduce the cooperative model to assist the people in rebuilding their lives. It was a very courageous decision by two dedicated people!

January, 1994
El Salvador

We flew into San Salvador and were picked up by one of Stanley's staff and taken to our hotel, the Renaissance, which was quite modern and well appointed—warm showers, good beds, and excellent food. That was the last "gringo" creature comforts we would have in about a week! A van picked us up with our luggage at the hotel the next morning with the instructions that we were going to travel around the country to visit several agricultural cooperatives, and then arrive at Perquin, in Morazon, in northeastern El Salvador. The country is one of the smallest in Latin America (21,393 sq. kilometers; or 8,260 sq. miles), and one of the most dense with a population of about eight and a half million people. Stanley wanted our group to spend most of our time in Morazon, named "El Gigante" for several reasons: this was the mountainside community, which was the site of the largest massacre of civilians by Salvador's federal troops in modern Latin American history. The casualties were mainly women and children and it was estimated that about four thousand were killed! The men, of course, were fighting the troops elsewhere, so the troops, with destructive firepower, took advantage of their absence to destroy, by way of their reconnaissance, everyone who was left at home.

Another reason for this particular venue was that Stanley wanted us to meet several of the women and children who had survived, which was important to the development of the cooperative. That is, several women hid in secret hiding places which had been prepared for such an attack. As the troops left one part of the area, the women would come out of their hiding place and shoot several troops, then hurriedly flee to the mountainside where they knew the terrain better than the troops. The "Federales" couldn't spend too much time looking for them in that they didn't know when the men of the village would return. When the men did return, they were first horrified, then astounded that their wives, sisters, and mothers had engaged and killed the aggressors! These women, then, had achieved equal status with the men in a highly macho society. That equal status would later translate, into women holding key, management responsibilities in the developing cooperative.

Because of the climatic conditions (relatively high altitude, and cool, damp nights), the primary crop that the cooperative began to grow and harvest was coffee. It was not ordinary coffee, but organic coffee, for organic coffee demanded a 30 percent premium on the open market. This product could be labeled "organic" because no chemical fertilizers had been used for many years, because of the civil war. Early the following year, I met with an officer of Starbucks, and he indicated that if El Gigante could grow and harvest a container of organic coffee, Starbucks would buy it; and he did! To sustain themselves, the coop members also grew vegetables, including lettuce, carrots, tomatoes and melons, while raising chickens and pigs for protein, and in the true coop model, shared the production, harvesting and, in the future, the proceeds from the sale of those commodities. Stanley and Gloria and their local staff had initiated hope for the people of Morazon, who, in turn, turned that precious quality into a thriving business through their hard work, and enterprising spirit.

January 1995
El Salvador

My wife, Ellen, and I returned to El Salvador early in 1995, and as part of my job with NCBA/CLUSA, I was required to report on the progress of the activities there to the US Agency for International Development and the US Department of Agriculture, the funding agencies for our work there. These agencies offered RFP's (Requests for Proposals) and CLUSA and other NGO's (Non Governmental Agencies) submitted responses based upon how we assessed the needs of the country of record. More often than not, CLUSA was successful in obtaining the grant for work to be accomplished in a designated period of time, not only in El Salvador, but throughout the world where help was needed. The primary reason for this success was that CLUSA had a cadre of excellent contractual staff, many of whom had been Peace Corps graduates. These individuals had to perform in a country, often under dangerous circumstances, and therefore knew how to get things done. In addition, often, we selected individuals for these assignments whom had language skills related to the project at hand. During this period in the 1990's, the United States was extremely focused on providing support to Latin and South America, countries that had gone through turmoil, economic instability, and civil war.

Ellen was able to make the trip with me, not only because she could speak Spanish, but her teaching schedule as a professor at Johns Hopkins University, at home, had not yet started. In addition, during our first visit, in 1994, we learned that when we asked the question of the members of many cooperatives, "What is your greatest need?", the answer was always, without exception, "Education for our children." They continued, "We need Spanish books, we need schools, we need teachers, because we don't want our children to grow up not able to read and write, like us." It hadn't occurred to us, that with a civil war of ten to twelve years, schools had been destroyed, and education was non-existent. The power structure of the country did not want the people to be educated, because the peons had provided cheap labor for many, many years. These responses, from the community interestingly, came before any mention of food, money or clothing. The people believed that education, for their children, especially, was the way out of poverty.

Stanley Kuehn met Ellen and I at the airport and wondered why we had so many boxes, including our luggage. We explained to him that we had brought books for all ages of children and when we explained to the airlines that we were bringing children's books to El Salvador, they did not charge us for the extra weight. We drove directly to Perquin, a village of about five hundred people in the state of Morazan in northwest El Salvador. The cooperative, which had been chartered, was named El Gigante. We were met by a group of children, whom Stanley had telephoned earlier, and they immediately opened the boxes of books and began looking at the pictures and trying to sound out several Spanish words. It was like a homecoming, and their enthusiasm was contagious. The village was in the middle stages of repair from the war, and the villagers were living in huts with thatched roofs, plywood and cane sides, and wooden bed frames elevated slightly off the ground, to avoid dampness. Cooking was done in a large, open air thatched pavilion using charcoal, wood, and a large grill-all community style. The women of the village took turns preparing meat, vegetables and fruit. Picnic tables provided sit down space, but, there was no designated place for the books to be sheltered from the elements—a library was not high on the priority list of the coop! We had an opportunity to spend some time with the staff during this trip, and to estimate progress of our mission, which was to develop sustainable coop businesses in keeping with the RFP's that had funded our grants for El Salvador.

Carolina Sanchez was Stan's key administrator, secretary, and co-ordinator. She was vivacious, positive and very competent woman of young middle age. Leon Padilla was the assistant manager to Stan and handled the coordination of supplies among the cooperatives which had been begun by Stan and the crew, also in his twenties. There were many others, including Leon's brother, Carlos, Jaime Santana and a host of workers who were out in the field every day, managing the production of the crops, which included cashews, coffee, and market garden fruits and vegetables.

November, 1996
El Salvador

We returned to El Salvador in the fall of 1996, accompanied by a group of Nationwide Insurance Directors, most of whom were also Directors of NCBA/CLUSA. Included were Arden and Clarice Shisler, Henry and Barbara Holloway, and Bob and Gwen Stewart and Bill and Helen Swank. As Chairman of the Nationwide Board, Arden wanted to see, first hand, what we were doing in the country, so that he could provide specific information to the entire Nationwide Board upon his return. This was a courageous venture for these people, in that most had not been close to a civil war zone which was still in the simmering stages. Even though the peace accords had been signed, long memories of the war still existed on both sides of the conflict. Revenge was still ever-present in the minds of many. Several examples were noted in our initial briefings: a general, who had been in charge of the massacre at Perquin in the state of Morazon, mysteriously had his helicopter crash on a routine trip; a leader of the resistance, who was known to have attacked military convoys, was apprehended on a rural road, and had his throat cut; and back and forth, the cycle continued of killing and payback. It was in this context that our visit began.

We were invited, the first evening, to an outdoor café in San Salvador, which was decorated with multi-colored hanging lights, picnic benches, and music from a small group of men playing guitars, mouth pipes and violins. The Council of newly formed Cooperatives was intent on demonstrating that they were very pleased that a delegation from Nationwide would travel to their country and they provided cerveza (beer), chorizo (sausage), baby back ribs cooked over an open grill, and an array of fruits and vegetables. Tortillas with cheese, chicken, and somosas (a small, breaded snack), and guacamole were readily available. Several toasts were made and a good time was enjoyed by everyone. That night, we stayed in a modern hotel in the capital city. The next morning, we were scheduled to be briefed by the US Embassy staff before we started the tour of cooperatives. All of us were taken to the embassy in several of the SUV's which Stanley Kuehn used for the project, and we noted that each had a guard with an AK-47 at his side. At the gates of the embassy, the guards got out, and handed over their weapons, and concrete barriers were raised to prevent the vehicles from moving forward. Uniformed guards with portable mirrors approached each vehicle, checking underneath to ensure no bombs or explosive devices existed. Each passenger was asked for their passport, and it was checked before the barriers were lowered. We finally entered the grounds and approached the building where the briefing would be held. Security was extremely tight, indicating to us the continuing fear of reprisal!

El Salvador was a beautiful country with light sand beaches, rain forests, mountains, and even extinct volcanoes. There were several large calderas where volcanoes had erupted and left their "debris". Because of the rich soil near several of these calderas, farming and market gardening, coffee growing and the production of peanuts and cashews had been the most prominent of the cooperatives' initiatives. Because of the Civil War, tourism was almost non-existent, which we thought was a shame because of the lure of the beautiful beaches. Outside of the capital, the country was primarily agricultural, with very little exploration having been started to determine if "hard" commodities could be developed for export. We were taken to downtown El Salvador, to the offices of the Coop Council where we were briefed on the cooperatives on our schedule for the next several days. Those coops included El Gigante, Coralama, San Rafael de Los Naranjos, Santa Adelaida, UCRA-PROBEX,(the Union of Agrarian Reform Coops producers, and Exporters), and PROEX-SAL(Producers and Exporters of El Salvador). We were in for a busy week! We would be staying in and around those coops, not in a modern hotel! Before breaking for lunch, we met Pastora Rodriguez, who was one of the women who fought the Federales in Perquin. She was dressed in a business suit and *did not* look like an individual who would know how to handle a rifle. The next day, during our first trip into the field, we learned that she was a significant leader of the cooperative *and*, a formidable fighter.

November, 1996
EL Salvador

Our group was taken back to the US Embassy the next morning where we boarded a helicopter made available to us through the good graces of the embassy, which confirmed to us, that cooperative successes in the country were being recognized. It was a sunny, but very windy day and there was some doubt that we should make the trip up in the mountains, with forty mile an hour wind gusts. The forecast was that the winds would diminish, and that the trip was a "go". It became an hour long wild ride! As we approached the field which was level enough for us to set down, we noticed about one hundred men and women standing in a semi-circle, some with machetes, others with rifles, and handguns, and several, including women, had cartridge belts of bullets draped across their chests! We had understood that the embassy would let the villagers know of our arrival, but apparently, the message was either delayed or communication lines had been knocked out by the winds! My wife, Ellen, was next to the door of the helicopter and was first out the door, which was quite brave, given the circumstances, in that the winds were causing the 'copter to buck up and down. When you exited from a 'copter, it was necessary to keep your head down and to get out from under the blades as quickly as possible, which Ellen did. Also, the menacing group began to move forward as she exited! Ellen moved toward the group and was met about midway by Pastora Rodriguez, whom we had met yesterday, and Ellen had spent several minutes talking with her about children's education. Pastora was decorated with the cartridge belts which we had seen from the air, and did not look, at all, like the professional woman we had met the day before!

The two women embraced and talked briefly, while the rest of us exited from the helicopter. When the villagers saw the two women meet and talk, they lowered their weapons and ran to greet the rest of the group. As we learned, later, the Federales had come by helicopter when the massacre had occurred several years earlier, and because of the continuing tensions in the country, the villagers were taking no chances. All of our group understood immediately, in a new and dramatic way, just how much this village had endured during the Civil War! We were to witness even more of the devastation, as we toured the village later in the day. We were taken to the community dining area, which was a large thatched-roof, open air, dirt floor building with large wooden tables, and picnic style benches. Stanley Kuehn introduced us to the leaders of the cooperative and interpreted their answers to our questions as we discussed their successes, problems and needs. Several of the villagers did speak some broken English and several of our group spoke a smattering of Spanish, so the communication went well. We were given tea and water for a refreshment, then walked through the main portion of the village to view several of the huts which had not been destroyed during the raid. We had an opportunity to see the trap doors, which had been built so that the women and children could hide underneath if it was set on fire. Several had earthen exits leading to the jungle as another means of escape. Several huts had been left in burned-out condition, with machine gun holes and artifacts from the family who lived there, as a reminder to the villagers, and visitors like us, as to the extent of the massacre. It was a very sobering scene. At the edge of the village was a huge crater, about fifteen feet deep, which had been caused by a mortar shell fired by the Federales. The villagers had collected hand grenades, shrapnel from the attack, discarded rifles, etc. as well as newspaper articles from Latin America, the United States, and all over the world which described the massacre. The villagers had used one of the huts as a museum to display all of their memorabilia. None of us had ever witnessed such a display!

January, 1997
El Salvador
Ellen and I returned to El Salvador in early 1997, accompanied by a group of NCBA Board of Directors, and Paul Hazen, Vice President of NCBA. We knew that it would be our last official visit there because the terms of the project would be completed later that year. We wanted the board members to be able to confirm to the remaining members, at the next board meeting, their impressions and the progress of El Gigante and other cooperatives in El Salvador. The visiting members included Arden and Clarice Shisler, Gwen and Bob Stewart. We visited several of the cooperatives we had previously visited the year before, which included Colarama, San Rafael de Los Naranjos, and Santa Adelaida. We were impressed with the progress and the continued commitment which the villagers demonstrated and maybe most importantly, the expressions of pride in their work and their accomplishments! We were always

treated graciously, and were amazed regarding the understanding of the cooperative principles that had been incorporated into their daily lives. For example, we ventured far up the mountainside from El Salvador to Santa Adelaida, a land reform cooperative which demonstrated the importance of people joining together to allocate hectares of land for growing fruits and vegetables which were produced and sold through the auspices of the coop. In El Salvador, we returned to UCRA-PROBEX to witness the business operations of the coffee production rating and ranking system. Coffee was a universally accepted product, but the selection of the coffee beans into dark, medium and lighter grades, and the duration of the roasting process were essential to the acceptance of the product on the world market. Also, as mentioned earlier, because there had been no chemical fertilizer or pesticides used on the old coffee plants or the fields where the coffee was grown for many years, a large portion of the yield could be identified as "organic", which commanded a premium price on the world market. The coffee brand name was PEPIL. In one of our earlier visits, we noted the need for books, at all reading levels, which were written in Spanish. We had brought several boxes of books at that time, but it was cumbersome and costly. We discussed this issue with Stanley and Gloria Kuehn and several of the leaders of the individual coops, as well as the need for some place to store the books. With the help of our Nationwide/NCBA Directors, Ellen and I took the lead and committed to raise funds for a library at El Gigante, which would be built by the members of the coop and would be available to other coops in El Salvador. In addition, we said that if we could raise enough funds, then the excess could be used to purchase books. We returned to the United States, and began our fundraising efforts, beginning with NCBA members, Nationwide Directors of NCBA, friends, relatives, and interested people. Initially, we raised over $5,000 and sent the funds through the Cooperative Development Foundation to Stanley and Gloria in El Salvador. In the interim, Stan and the coop leadership had begun drawing up plans, and the coops had started to manufacture clay bricks which would be used for the building—much more substantial than many of the huts which were still being used for living! In less than a year, the building was finished and, because of the continuing flow of funds, the project had grown from just a library into a community center! Ellen's mother, Mary Elms, had died in 1994, and Ellen asked Stanley and the coop leaders if the library section of the building could honor her memory, which they unanimously agreed. The plaque, outside the library reads:

BIBLIOTECA "EL RINCON DEL LIBRO" en honor a MARY ALICE ELMS, 1912-1994. Quien amo a odos Los Ninos Del Muncie; COOPERATIVA EL GIGANTE, Perquin, El Salvador, C. A. November, 1997.

The translation is: "This corner library is in honor of Mary Alice Elms, who loves all the children of the world." Since that time, the center has added a medical office/small clinic which was staffed on a part-time basis, and was truly the focal point of celebrations in the community. I retired from NCBA/CBI the following year but the memories of our work in El Salvador would remain with Ellen and me for the rest of our lives.

1995
Earthquake

Kobe, Japan,

In early March, 1995, I received a letter from Shigenori Takemoto, President and CEO of the Japanese Consumers' Cooperative Union (JCCU), and Chairman of Co-op Kobe indicating he had read about NCBA's efforts, along with the U.S. cooperative community to raise funds, and clothing for the Kobe earthquake victims. *The New York Times*, in a February issue, called the earthquake which occurred on January 17, 1995, "the most expensive natural disaster in the history of man—about $120 billion [US dollars] in damages!" That figure paled in comparison to the human cost of deaths and injuries.

Over six thousand people had died, and thirty thousand-plus were injured. That spring, over one hundred thousand people were living in temporary refugee areas in and around Kobe, in tents, small trailers, and pre-fabricated housing units which were designed for no more than four people. The earthquake had registered 7.2 on the Richter scale, among the highest readings ever recorded. The city of Kobe, with a population of about one million, five hundred thousand and the sur-rounding prefecture of Hyogo, was heavily damaged and water, elec-tricity, sewer—the basic services—were not functioning. The Coop Headquarters was completely demolished, and administrative functions had been moved to Kyodogakuen, the Coop College and Life Cultural Center, outside of Kobe, which had suffered some damage, but was operational. The fact that President Takemoto took the time to write to me was an indication of the need of the people of Kobe.

The earthquake had killed eleven coop employees, and forty-eight family members of coop employees. Mr. Takemoto indicated that about 70 percent of the households in the affected area were members of the Kobe Co-op. Of the one hundred and fifty-five retail stores in the coop, four were demolished, and thirty-five severely damaged. It was estimated that fifty-five billion yen (over five hundred million US dollars) would be required for getting the Kobe Coop operational. Of course, because insurance coverage would be available to assist in some of the rebuilding efforts, it would be a very long time before any sense of "normal" would return to the coop and Kobe, itself. As I read President Takemoto's letter, I felt that the US cooperative community had to redouble our efforts to assist in any way possible. I sent letters to NCBA members, and the membership of the International Cooperative Alliance, the international body of cooperatives, which is headquartered in Geneva, Switzerland. My letter requested money, which was easily transferable, and clothing, food, water, etc. that could be sent to Japan, directly. It was obviously more expensive to send heavy items, but whatever was available was certain to be appreciated.

Many organizations responded, and I'll list only a few of them to indicate examples of the outpouring of assistance. The Twin Pines Foundation, headed by David Thompson, in California; the Cooperative Development Foundation, under the NCBA organizational structure; the National Cooperative Bank, headed by Charles Snyder; the Student Housing Coop, headed by Jim Jones; and REI (Recreational Equipment, Inc.) headed by Wally Smith. Nationwide Insurance's President, Dimon McPherson, was adamant about sending funds immediately to the Kobe Co-op. With these efforts and those of the international community, President Takemoto sent me a personal invitation to bring funds, and greetings from the US Coop community and to come to Kobe for the Annual Meeting of the Kobe Cooperative. No one had ever been asked from outside of the coop community in Japan to speak at their annual meeting!

I obviously didn't want to use the funds collected for the Kobe Relief Fund to travel to Japan, but one of the Nationwide Directors had funded an international support fund, called the Frank Sollars Fund, which was included in the Cooperative Foundation's series of international funds. He immediately suggested my airfare could be paid by that fund. As it turned out, even the use of a CDF Fund, was not necessary. When I called Northwest Airlines to make my reservation, I explained that I was going on "a mission of mercy" to Kobe, Japan, and I was referred to a Northwest officer in Minneapolis. He asked about my planned trip, and indicated that Northwest would like to participate in this relief effort. He said that Northwest would fly my wife, Ellen, and I first class to San Francisco, where we would be met by a Northwest representative. Our itinerary took us from Washington, D.C. to San Francisco and we changed planes to go to Osaka, Japan. There, we were met by a representative of the Kobe Co-op, and we were to go by train to Kobe. We had to stay at a hotel in Osaka, because of the horrific damage in Kobe. Northwest had also arranged for our hotel in Osaka. Amazing!

As we approached Kobe by train, we were overwhelmed by the devastation of this once, beautiful city. The earthquake had ruptured natural gas lines which resulted in raging fires throughout the city. Many Japanese homes were built with bamboo and wooden screens and those homes became kindling to feed the fire. Railroad ties also contributed to the fire and rails were twisted and bent in grotesque shapes, some as high as eight to ten feet in the air, almost like surreal sculptures. Civic buildings such as police stations, libraries and courthouses were severely damaged or non-existent. Some had the front of the building still standing, but nothing more! As far as we could see, over the horizon, were large blue tarpaulins flapping in the breeze, covering some part of individual buildings designed to keep the elements out, and provide some privacy. This "sea of blue" was a metaphor in our eyes, of the depression which many people must have experienced, who had survived this terrible event. On the other hand, many of the pre-fabricated units which President Takemoto had described in his letter, had tricycles, small swing sets, and sand boxes outside, indicating that children were enjoying life and the parents were ensuring that the kids were trying to be "normal". The toys gave us the impression that nothing could defeat the people of this city! Also, we noticed a number of the units had tortoise shells hanging outside the entrance. We were told that these shells were considered icons to keep evil spirits away. Finally, we saw signs in Japanese that said, "SOGANI", which meant "it can't be helped"!

President Takemoto met us as we entered the college, and took us to one of the lunchrooms where we were offered tea and a snack. He gave us a quick tour, then took us to his office and provided a review of tomorrow's events, starting with the Annual Meeting of Co-op Kobe. He wanted me to present the check of $50,000 to him on behalf of the US cooperative movement, and then say a few words, introducing Ellen, and bringing greetings and support, and hope to the delegates. Obviously, this was quite an honor for me and as I discovered this was unprecedented as far as Co-op Kobe was concerned. We returned to our hotel in Osaka, and were met the next morning by our coop friend who took us to the train and back to Kobe. The president introduced me and I presented the check to him, and then I briefly spoke a few words of greeting, and concluded with a quote from Oscar Arias, former President of Costa Rica, and a significant supporter of cooperatives: "Hope is the strongest force which moves people. A hope that transforms, that makes new realities, is that which opens the way of liberty to man. To encourage hope, it is necessary to unite courage and knowledge in all people". Finally, I noted that Dr. Toyohiko Kagawa, one of the early pioneers of cooperation, worldwide, had brought a message of hope to the United States in the late 1920's and 1930's, the latter during the terrible Great Depression. He had a huge impact in our country, and was honored with a statue in the Washington D.C.

National Cathedral, the only cooperative member to be so honored. After my comments the translator completed her job so the delegates [about 2,000], could hear my final words, on their translation devices.

Absolute silence followed, then all of a sudden, everyone stood up and applauded and cheered! I was astonished, and I believed President Takemoto was, also. The proper, reserved members, who had been through so much, wanted to show their appreciation and enthusiasm for the support of the US cooperative community. The president came over to me and gave me a big bear hug, and asked Ellen to join me on the dais and she received more applause! David Thompson, mentioned earlier, was with us and he was to meet later with the coop housing group to determine how assistance could be provided for new housing for Kobe. President Takemoto took Ellen and me back to his office and had tea and cookies ready for our morning snack, and a break following the annual meeting. We discussed his early background during World War II and we responded with our memories and how it had affected our lives. I had inquired from our guide, the day before, and learned that President Takemoto's favorite cocktail was Johnny Walker Black Label Scotch, which at that time, I bought two bottles. Then, in his office during our discussion, I presented him with our gift, thanking him for all his hospitality. He was very pleased with our gift, and invited us to take a tour of several of the co-op's retail stores before going to lunch. We were taken by his private car to three stores which reminded us of the large Kohl's or Target stores in the US. They contained fresh vegetables, fresh fish and Kobe beef, sushi, lox, and several floors of furniture, draperies, carpeting, etc. It confirmed to Ellen and to me, the preeminence of the Kobe Co-op brand in this part of Japan, but the surprises continued. Each time we entered a store, we were met by the store manager, and several assistants, who took us to the first of many television screens throughout the store which featured my comments to the Kobe Annual Meeting in Japanese. The President had arranged to have tapes made of our comments at the meeting while we were in his office, then distributed them throughout the Kobe Co-Op stores! I knew then that the Kobe Co-Op would be on its feet in very quick order, with that kind of organization! We were obviously very pleased and impressed with his gesture.

We stayed in Kobe for another day and a half and enjoyed the company of President Takemoto and also tasted Kobe beef, which was melt-in-your-mouth delicious! He had arranged for a quick trip to Kyoto, the original capital of Japan, to tour the ancient Heran Shrine, which was regarded as a Shinto Holy Place, and included a fifty-three foot statue of Buddha, one of the world's tallest replicas. After that visit, we took the bullet train back to Tokyo to catch our flight to San Francisco, courtesy of Northwest Airlines. We traveled on to Washington, D.C. and carried the "Kobe spirit" of determination and hope back with us and reported all of our experiences to the NCBA Board of Directors and the US Cooperative community. Ellen and I have never forgotten the commitment of the cooperative spirit of Kobe to honor their dead, to re-build their lives, and to re-double their efforts in making Co-Op Kobe the very best example of what cooperatives were all about, serving members in good times and in bad times!

International Cooperative Alliance
Centennial Anniversary
Manchester, England
1995

Background
The ICA was headquartered in Geneva, Switzerland and was regarded as the membership clearing house for cooperative ideas and programs throughout the world. The ICA, periodically, brought together cooperative leaders from all over the world to share information and, to discuss solutions to problems that otherwise might be relegated to a one on one discussion between countries. For example, in India, a milk pasteurization coop had developed a country-wide number of refrigerated collection stations for farmers to bring their fresh milk for processing and distribution. This innovation, as simple as it sounds, was a vast improvement over the farmers having to drive miles and miles to deliver their milk. In El Salvador, farmers grow coffee beans in higher elevations which had not been treated with chemical fertilizers. The farmers could then designate that the beans and the resulting coffee were organic, thereby obtaining a premium price.

Few people realize that of the world's population in the 21st century of almost seven billion, nearly one-third are members of cooperatives! Now, there is some double counting in that figure because some people are members of several cooperatives such as rural electrics, credit unions, and agricultural marketing coops. But the financial impact by cooperatives on the world economy is significant… and growing. Co-operatives' members pay taxes on their share earnings, and cooperatives employ thousands of people who, in turn, pay taxes on their individual earnings. Products and services produced by cooperatives are meeting members' needs, and of course, smaller cooperatives utilize volunteers which keep expenses low. The ICA, essentially, then, encourages cooperative development.

First Modern Cooperative and Centennial Anniversary

This historic meeting was held in Manchester to celebrate the 100th anniversary of the inception of the ICA, and to recognize the formation of the first successful modern consumer's cooperative, the Rochdale Equitable Pioneers Society. Manchester, in the late 1890's, was a bustling, industrial city of about twenty thousand people, and was regarded as a "labor city"; that is, a place where the Industrial Revolution was changing the relationship between labor, capital and management. In the center of Manchester, today, is the building designated as the Grain Exchange, which is now a museum depicting the struggles of laboring men and women; but in the 1890's, it was a focal point in the trade of agricultural products for the region. One of the trades which was important at that time was that of weavers, who worked for companies that bought cotton, and employed people to make clothing and other fabric-based products. These workers were paid only a subsistence wage, and were obliged to buy their food at company stores. A group of the weavers noticed that water was being added to the milk, and sawdust was being substituted for corn meal! These courageous men decided to open their own store to ensure that they could be certain that they were "getting what they paid for"!

The weavers had families, and children who were under-nourished and they lived in small shanty-like structures, most times unheated. The Co-Op store opened for business in one of these houses on December 21, 1894 for just two hours each day. The pioneers had saved pennies from their small pay in order to purchase basic items for sustenance—

butter, milk, flour, sugar, and oatmeal. The gas company would not provide light for them so they had to buy candles. The men took turns, after their working day, to open the store and handle the commerce. From this humble beginning, the concepts of membership, dividend payments, cooperatives principles, volunteerism, etc., all early concepts in the formation of a cooperative, came forward. The idea of cooperation had been realized to apply to small businesses, and was destined to continue to grow in England, in Europe, and finally, to be exported to the United States. The book, *Weavers of Dreams*, written by David Thompson, who was born in England, but now resides in California, had its 3rd printing in 1995. The book details the tremendous effort of the original group of weavers, in their quest for economic justice, social integration and recognition of the value of human labor.

I was privileged to lead the US Delegation to this centennial celebration, which lauded the contributions of the ICA and the recognition of the first successful consumer cooperative. In addition, there was the necessary attention provided to proposed changes in the accepted cooperative principles by the world-wide membership, and the concern about sustainable human development in underdeveloped countries in the 21st century. Finally, it was agreed that, in addition to the six cooperatives principles, a 7th principle would be added—concern for community. (These seven principles are noted in the forward of this memoir.) The ICA Congress was sent a letter by the Secretary-General of the United Nations at that time, which stated:

> As we move into a new millennium, the partnership between the United Nations and the ICA becomes increasingly important...They [cooperatives] constitute a model for people-centered and a sustainable form of societal organization, based in equity, justice and solidarity.

During our several days in Manchester, one day, after lunch, my wife, Ellen, and I took a walk prior to the business meetings which started in the afternoon. We turned a corner into a small plaza, and we were greeted by a ten foot statue of President Abraham Lincoln! *What was a statue of our US President doing in Manchester, England?* we asked ourselves. At the base of the statue, was affixed a bronzed plaque which had recently been polished. The plaque indicated that this statue had been erected after Lincoln's death by the mill workers and people of Manchester in recognition of Lincoln's promise during the Civil War, that the United States would continue to buy uniforms, and processed cotton goods, from Manchester, even after the war was over. The promise had been made because the Confederacy had blockaded ships from England, shipping all manner of goods to the United States, with the prospect that the economic hardship on the workers in Manchester, and all of England, would force them to join forces against the Union! Obviously, workers lost their jobs or were put on half pay, and the British economy suffered. The Union won, of course, but the Union administration kept President Lincoln's promise and the workers in Manchester never forgot it! Our discovery was another one of those serendipitous moments, when, in the midst of an important world-wide meeting of cooperatives, the enduring relationship between the United States and Great Britain was again, confirmed.

EPILOGUE

As I continue to enjoy retirement, mainly engaging in volunteer areas of interest, my wife, Ellen, and I also still continue to look forward to traveling, internationally. We have taken Spanish lessons in Cuernavaca, Mexico and helped children with medical problems in Nicaragua. We both had worked overseas during our careers, yet the lure of learning about different cultures, and meeting people who look and think differently from our local friends and neighbors continues to be a siren-song, beckoning us to seek out new countries to explore.

Several years ago, I decided to write a memoir, and one of the many reasons to do so was the universal truth that cooperatives represent an unusual combination of idealism and realism. Idealism, in that the prospect of "something better" in the lives of people involved in a cooperative; hope for educational opportunities for children, and the participation and bonding that results in any cooperative venture. Realism, in that people all over the world need food, clothing and shelter, and cooperatives are essentially economic enterprises—not-for-profit small businesses that may become even larger. These enterprises must produce products and or services that have value, and can produce earnings for the cooperative and its members.

My memoir includes many journeys which reflect the combination of idealism and realism which I experienced in my working life. Two of the more important of these journeys occurred in El Salvador and Indonesia. Now, in 2016, I wanted to know how cooperatives were doing, in these two important countries.

EL Salvador

The cooperative model was a perfect fit for a war-torn country like El Salvador in the 1990's. The Civil War had claimed thousands of lives, and the need for a stable government which could help the people, economically, was paramount. The United States government and the Salvadoran government began to forge a positive partnership that promised work and opportunity to repair the country and its people. Cooperatives encompassed both of those objectives. Salvadorans wanted to earn a living, feel pride in their accomplishments and most of all, wanted educational opportunities for their children, many of whom had never been to school, and therefore reading and writing skills were non-existent. One of the primary reasons that El Salvador began its healing process was that Stanley & Gloria Kuehn , working in conjunction with USAID, the US development agency, immediately established a working relationship with people in multiple locations. In effect, they said, "We want to work with you, but to do that effectively, the village leaders must discuss with us what you think will work best for you." Stanley *did not* say, "Here is what we are going to do." The people in each village had to buy in with their respective opinions, and it worked. Through their efforts of building trust, giving credit to local leadership, and establishing plans and programs geared to the unique locations of each cooperative, at the beginning of the 21st century, there were sixty-five successful cooperatives in the country.

The Kuehns left El Salvador at that time for another assignment, and their departure coincided with an influx of Salvadoran gang members who had been deported from the United States, especially from the West Coast. These young men had traveled to the US to find work, and when that option was closed, they began illegal activities of all kinds: extortion, murder, drugs, theft, etc. These gangs became even better organized in their home country, and began to exert pressure on all types of businesses, including cooperatives for payment for protection; that is, extortion. A recent article in *The Economist*, May 21, 2016, indicated that about 16 percent of the gross domestic product of the country is being siphoned off by the gangs. The article estimated that 25 percent of the population of the country is in the age range of fifteen to twenty-nine, most of whom are not working, nor are they in school! Therefore, one primary option is becoming a gang member. The Salvadoran government has not invested in education on a nation-wide basis, nor has the government developed work projects that would address the problem of idle time of this age group. A law that would support these programs has been stalled in the legislature for six years!

Stanley and Gloria Kuehn recently returned to El Salvador, as Chief of Party, for NCBA/CLUSA, working with the US Department of Agriculture to attempt to re-energize many of the cooperatives which they worked so hard to develop in the 1990's. They have initiated the Coffee Rehabilitation and Agricultural Diversification Project designed to support five thousand coffee growers to overcome the coffee rust crises, and begin shipping Pipil coffee,(the brand name), once again to stores in the US and in other world markets. The challenge for Stanley and Gloria is different in 2016, but certainly just as difficult as the devastation of the Civil War which they helped to overcome in the 1990's.

Indonesia

Indonesia's government has experienced several leadership changes, since my journeys there. As mentioned earlier, President Suharto was overthrown in 1998, and Suslio Bambang Yudhoyone became the country's first directly elected president in 2014. His successor, Joko Widdo, the former Mayor of Solo, a town in Northern Jakarta, and the recent Governor of Jakarta was recently elected President. He has no ties to the army or parliament, and comes from humble circumstances, which has made him attractive to the people. Throughout these political changes, Sam Filiaci and his staff have continued to innovate and work with the leaders of the local cooperatives on the various islands where he found opportunities. In this country, success has bred success, and the government, even through the political changes mentioned above, has supported cooperatives. It is significant that Sam and his family have lived there permanently, and his staff *and* the government are very much aware of his commitment. In addition to the vanilla bean and other spices which the cooperatives have produced and marketed, the cooperatives have fashioned mahogany, teak and bamboo furniture which have been exported all over the world. Several other significant developments have taken place as I reviewed developments in Indonesia in 2016. They include:

- Twenty thousand workers are employed by the cooperatives, serving thousands of farm families. Their labors have produced and exported hundreds of millions of US dollars worth, mainly of agricultural products.
- Cooperatives and their international partners have implemented critical social programs, including: building several dozen health clinics; providing health care services with two point two million patient visits; building and operating several dozen water and sanitation facilities; implementing relief programs for natural disaster and conflict victims in several areas of the country; and building and operating numerous educational institutions, from pre-kindergarten to higher education facilities.

This summary of the impact of cooperatives in Indonesia, over the years in which Sam Filiaci has demonstrated his leadership, indicates achievement at the highest level. I am very proud to have been associated, in a small measure, with all that Sam has accomplished through and with cooperatives, there.

Text References

AFRICA ADORNED, Angela Fisher, Harry N. Abrams, Inc., New York, 1989

BRAZIL, Insight Guide, Langenscheidt Publications, Inc., New York, 2000

COLUMBIA ENCYCLOPEDIA, 6th Edition, 2000

EL SALVADOR, Background Notes, United States State Department, Office of Public Communications, Vol. IV., No. 2, February, 1993

INDONESIA, People and Histories, Jean Gelman Taylor, Yale University Press, 2003

KOBE, A Visual History of the Kobe Earthquake, Kobe International Association, 1995

LESSONS FROM EL SALVADOR'S TRAGEDY, The Economist, PP. 31, January 30, 2001

MURRAY D. LINCOLN, "A Man Who Made a Difference", Nationwide Insurance Company, 75thAnniversary Publication, Columbus, Ohio, April 12, 2001

PRESIDENT'S COMMENTS, Cooperative Business Journal, Washington, D.C., 1993-1998

STRANGER AT THE GATE, [a novel of Indonesia], Malcolm Bosse, Simon and Shuster, 1989

WEAVERS OF DREAMS, Founders of the Modern Cooperative Movement, Center for Cooperatives, University of California, Davis, David J. Thompson, 1995

WHEN KOBE DIED, Time Magazine, PP. 24-33, Vol. 145, No. 4, January 30, 1995

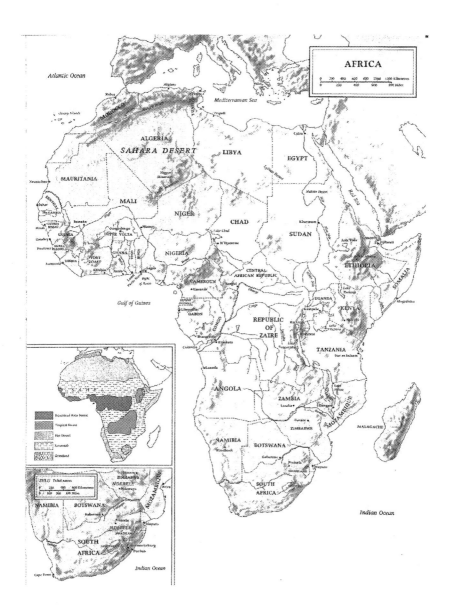

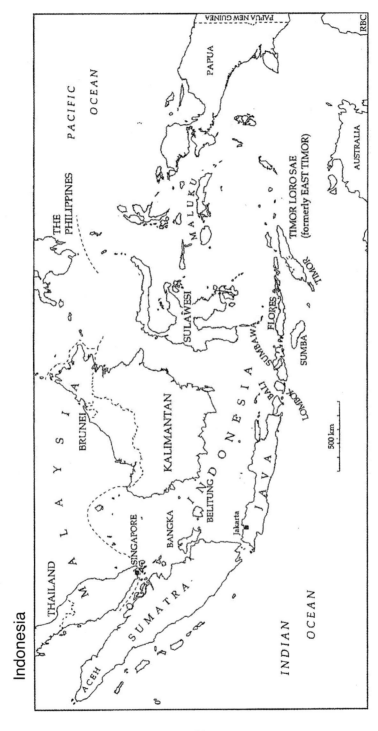

Indonesia

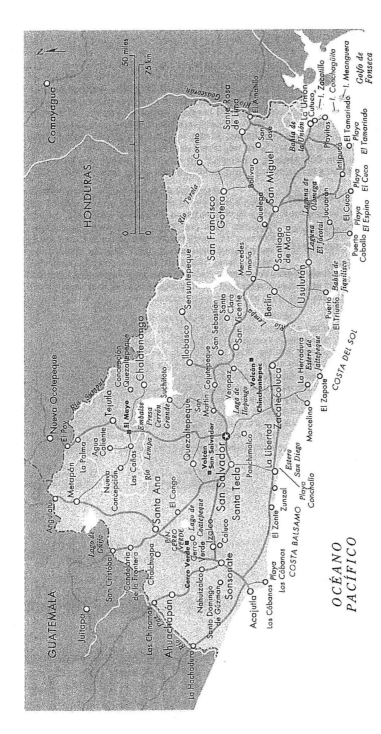

El Salvador

EL SALVADOR